TATE MODERN
BUILDING A MUSEUM FOR THE 21st CENTURY

Edited by Chris Dercon and Nicholas Serota

Tate Publishing

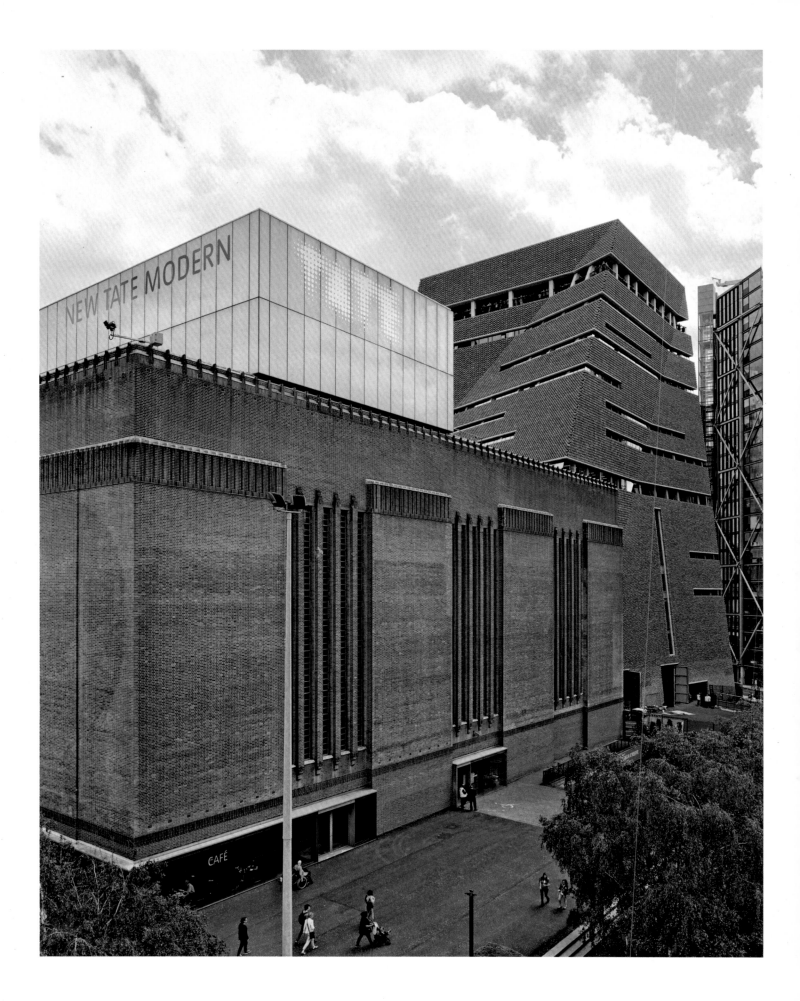

Contents

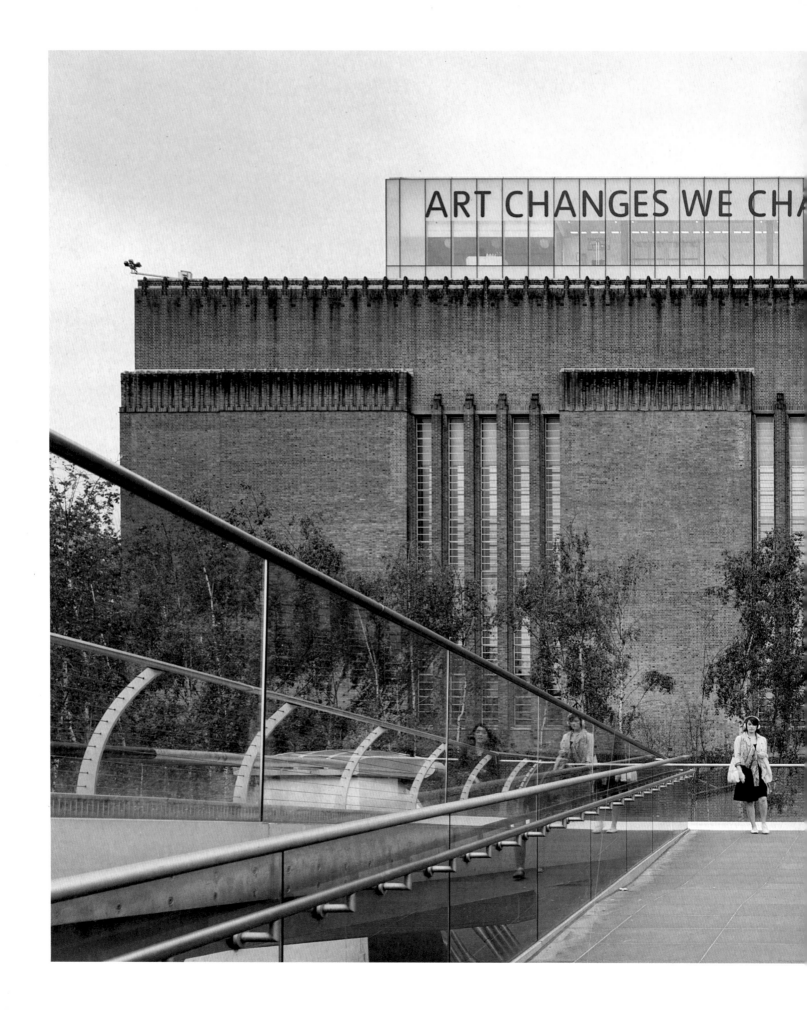

Aerial view of Tate Modern, May 2016.

Nicholas Serota
Foreword

Museums both reflect and express the values of society. Tate Modern is no exception, and the creation of a museum of modern and contemporary art for London at the end of the twentieth century has been conditioned by long-standing attitudes to contemporary art in Britain, by a changing perception of Britain's place in the world, and by a recognition that a conventional history of modern art that is centred on Paris before 1945, and especially on New York in the post-war period, can no longer be sustained.

The Tate Modern building has been created in two campaigns with design phases occurring in 1995–7 and 2006–9. Most museums grow over time, but, most unusually, the extension of Tate Modern has been designed by the same team of architects and curators that designed the original building. Each phase is a response to the evolving experience and needs of Tate Modern, expressed in an increasingly complex architectural language that has developed through a decade of commissions across the world. In 1994 when Herzog & de Meuron won the competition to design Tate Modern their work was known only to a small number of architectural enthusiasts beyond their native Switzerland, where they had built some innovative apartments, industrial, office and domestic buildings, and one small pavilion for a private collection in Munich. By 2006 when they were selected to design the second phase of Tate Modern, again in competition, they had designed the Olympic stadium in Beijing, the de Young Museum in San Francisco, and the Walker Art Center in Minneapolis, and had been awarded the Pritzker Prize. The success of the original Tate Modern was one springboard for this success. In the second phase the architects have returned to a familiar, if much changed, location and have enjoyed a rare opportunity to create a building in dialogue with their own work. The result is a single building with contrasting elements that will stretch the idea of what a museum can offer a visitor.

During the early part of the nineteenth century the continental European royal collections were opened to the population as a whole. New, often free, public institutions, such as the British Museum which opened in 1753, grew out of an enthusiasm for collecting objects and classifying knowledge, and a belief that access to collections should be shared and not confined to specialists. In creating the buildings to house these collections, the Enlightenment model usually adopted the architectural language of classical Greece and Rome. Buildings were conceived as noble edifices in which the general population climbed the steps of the temple to escape the bustle of daily life and entered a sequence of grand halls and galleries illuminated by natural light from the glazed roofs above. Alongside these public rooms, scholars pursued inquiry in dedicated print and study rooms, later sharing their discoveries with interested audiences in public lectures.

In the early and mid-twentieth century, this model was adapted to the aspirations of a new class of collector, often living in houses designed by modernist architects of the same generation as the artists they were collecting. This more intimate scale is reflected in the rooms in Henry van de Velde's influential museum in Otterlo and in the traditional top-lit enfilade arrangement of the Kunstmuseum Basel (itself an important model for Herzog & de Meuron). In America, the new standard was established in 1939 by the Museum of Modern Art with Philip L. Goodwin and Edward Durell Stone's building in which there is a sequence of closed, artificially lit rooms on the scale of a New York apartment.

After the war a utopian belief that museums should attract a broad public found expression in buildings that were consciously designed to open themselves to the world, especially when they were built in rural or parkland locations. Notable amongst these were Otterlo, again, and Louisiana in Denmark, where galleries that include large windows are connected by perambulating walkways that allow the visitor to 'refresh' their eye by viewing nature as a relief from the intense experience of looking at art. This principle was also embraced by one of the most innovative directors of museums in the post-war period, Willem Sandberg, working with Gerrit Rietveld on the influential pavilion extension to the Stedelijk Museum (now demolished) which gave views onto the grass field of the *plein* but also the street in urban Amsterdam.

The idea of integrating the museum into its surroundings, allowing context to become an important part of the visitor experience, was given further impetus by Piano & Rogers at the Centre Pompidou in Paris in 1977. Elaborating on Cedric Price's influential idea of the 'Living City', Piano & Rogers reverted to the model of the mid-nineteenth-century market and exhibition hall with large open spaces divided by lightweight movable screens. Perimeter glass walls give views out onto the city. Such transparency, and the extended opening hours of the museum, broadcast a message that the museum should be a dynamic, living organism within the city.

However, the design of the Pompidou, with its flexibility and insubstantial interior architecture, did not anticipate the decisive shift in the sensibility of artists and curators that occurred in the 1960s with the move into film and video and the development of site-specific sculpture and installation that made use of warehouses and former industrial buildings. In both Europe and America new museums opened in former textile mills, such as the Crex Collection in Schaffhausen, Switzerland (1982), or in buildings like a former police garage in Los Angeles which became the 'Temporary Contemporary', associated with the newly founded Museum of Contemporary Art (1984). These buildings established a new model for the way in which contemporary art was shown and experienced, responding to the demands of artists for a seriousness and permanence that valued contemporary art as an equal of historic. Donald Judd's practice in installing work at his home in New York and especially in a series of buildings in Marfa, Texas, established a new paradigm.

When the Tate Trustees decided to adapt Giles Gilbert Scott's Bankside Power Station as the location for London's first museum of modern art in 1993 they were fully aware of the history and recent developments in the typology of museums. Amongst the Trustees were artists, such as Michael Craig-Martin and Bill Woodrow, whose network of international contacts and experience as exhibiting artists made them advocates for a building that would have the potential to offer both 'found' industrial space and refined galleries in which the early twentieth-century collection could be shown to advantage. Their view was powerfully reinforced by the answers given by fifty artists from across the world to a questionnaire seeking their comments on recent museum buildings in Europe and America. Almost without exception, they were critical of the modern and post-modern buildings that had been opened in the previous twenty years, favouring instead the late nineteenth and early twentieth-century Beaux-Arts buildings or those museums housed in former industrial buildings. Bankside was just such a space. Its huge volume offered an opportunity to create a range of conditions in which to show art, as well as the chance for growth in the future. But it also had the potential to change a city. Though the building was derelict and Bankside was off the map for most Londoners, it had great promise. It lay on the Thames directly opposite St Paul's Cathedral, and might even be connected to the City by a new footbridge. It was surrounded by land that could become a new green space in north Southwark and was not far distant from the Jubilee line that would open new connections to the east, west and north in 1998. It was the combination of these factors, and the determination to realise the full potential of the opportunity, not just for Tate but for London as a whole, that set the terms of the competition to select an architect in the summer of 1994.

The Trustees believed that the museum should be developed in collaboration with an architect, using the experience of artists and curators to generate and not simply to refine the design. The decision was therefore taken to select an architect rather than a scheme and to run a competition that would identify a team whose approach seemed to offer the greatest potential. Architects were invited to address three 'tasks' by setting out their proposals for the siting of the building in the urban context, for the way in which the building could accommodate the many public functions of a museum, and for the kind of galleries that could be formed through 'the imaginative use of natural daylight in a building on several floors'.

The selection of Herzog & de Meuron recognised their record of collaboration with artists, their imaginative decision to turn the Turbine Hall into a 'street' by opening it to its full depth, their restrained designs for galleries and their limited intervention in the symmetry of Scott's building. Their plan, conceived with landscape architects Kienast Vogt, to open routes and to create public space around the building was also admired. In the final design social and commercial space were accommodated in the lower floors and in the 'light beam' at the top, leaving the principal volumes of the Turbine Hall of the Boiler House for art. While the south lawns were left almost untouched, the area to the north along the river bank was extensively re-landscaped and planted with stands of birch to create a new park overlooking the Thames.

The unexpected public success of Tate Modern with 5.2 million visitors in the first year, the opening of the Millennium Bridge and an almost instant response from the more adventurous property developers, obliged Tate to consider development on the south side of Tate Modern much earlier than had originally been envisaged. Such were the pressures that there was a real anxiety that short-term profit might make it difficult to bring lasting benefit to the neighbourhood stretching south to Elephant and Castle. In 2001 the Trustees commissioned a 'Bankside Urban Study' from the Richard Rogers Partnership in an exercise led by Mike Davies. The purpose was to provide a framework for urban planning and improvements in the public realm that could be adopted by the planning authority and implemented over time by individual developers. The study confirmed the importance of establishing north-south pedestrian routes but also the value of creating small pockets of green space with high-quality planting and seating whenever an opportunity emerged in the planning process. Both principles were quickly adopted by Southwark and Transport for London. In 2007 Witherford Watson Mann were commissioned to develop their plans for 'Bankside Urban Forest', a proposal for a series of interventions in the public realm that by 2016 had resulted in more than twenty schemes within the neighbourhood.

In 2004 the Trustees decided to grasp another opportunity that had come earlier than anticipated. The arrival of a new generation of transformers allowed for the contraction of the UKPN (then EDF Energy) transformer facility into the eastern half of the Switch House. This opened up the possibility of creating a new south entrance to Tate Modern, a direct link between the Turbine Hall and the Tanks and additional spaces for overcrowded galleries, learning and social spaces. This time the brief was more straightforward, though the Trustees were determined that the building should set new standards in energy efficiency amongst museums. However, the site and its challenges were more complex, with constraints created by statutory controls designed to protect the views of St Paul's, the rights of neighbours, and a wish to preserve public space so recently given over to the community. A second competition with four shortlisted practices, Richard Rogers Partnership, Herzog & de Meuron, Dominique Perrault and Wilkinson Eyre, was won, slightly against the odds, by Herzog & de Meuron. This opened the way for further dialogue between a now more experienced client and architect. In the brief much was obvious – open up the south entrance, create a new public space looking south to Southwark, improve cafés, members rooms and shops for visitors. The challenge lay in the configuration of the spaces within a tight envelope, in the size and heights of gallery spaces that would contrast with the existing rooms in the Boiler House and in the treatment of the facade.

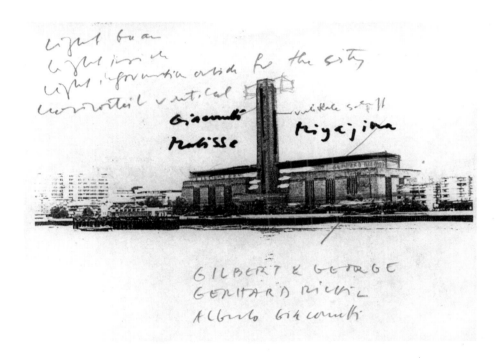

The starting point for the new building lay in the clover leaf form of the former oil tanks to the south of the Turbine Hall. These had always suggested the potential of creating a space for performance and installation that would be unique in the museum world. Indeed, so appealing was this idea that for a short period in 1997 the Trustees considered incorporating them in the first phase of the project, only to hold back through shortage of funds. Now they provided an inspiring foundation for the new building, the pyramidal form of which would be determined in part by the need to preserve statutory sightlines of St Paul's from other parts of the city.

Initially there was a strong desire to create separate galleries, each with its own individual character, a strategy used very successfully by SANAA at the 21st Century Museum of Contemporary Art in Kanazawa, Japan in 2004. Such 'rooms' soon became 'boxes' stacked and linked by a processional stair. In the initial design these boxes and the facade were clad in glass. However, following the economic recession, fundraising proceeded more slowly and this gave an opportunity to think again, both about the practicality of installing a large collection of art in separate volumes and also about the glass when so many of the surrounding commercial buildings were using the same material. Eventually, the galleries coalesced in a more conventional fashion onto the footprint of the original Switch House while retaining a variety of heights and sources of lighting. The facade was clad in a specially designed brick, chosen to complement Gilbert Scott's original variegated coloured brick.

The 'new' Tate Modern is not the 'old' Tate Modern with an extension, but a combination of elements clustered round the north-south route through the Turbine Hall and east-west axis of the 'street' of the Hall itself. Public and private functions lock together, as they do in a city. The galleries offer a complete repertoire of volumes, sizes and heights, with different forms of natural and artificial light. They are both refined and raw, while the Turbine Hall itself is a unique space in which artists can conceive work for a large audience. Tate Modern has become an instrument with many notes and tones in which the most intimate work can find a place, as well as the most grand.

Beyond the galleries, Tate Modern is a space for congregation, performance, debate, the exchange of ideas, the experience of the obsessions of others and the discovery of self. Museums have always been places of exploration. In the twenty-first century they are also places in which we can examine shared and contested values. Here in London, we have a long tradition of free access to institutions governed by trustees who hold the collection on behalf of the 'commoners' who are the ultimate owners. At a time of growing disparity of wealth in society, the creation of a great civic building is an expression of a belief in a 'commonwealth' of ideas. Herzog & de Meuron's building is a platform for ideas, but it has also been designed to shape our experience of the city, our appreciation of contemporary life and our understanding of ourselves.

A book marking the opening of such an ambitious project cannot be simply a promotion of an architectural monument. From the outset, Chris Dercon, Director of Tate Modern from 2011 to 2016, and I were determined that this book should not only reflect the views of those who commissioned the building, but also those who were involved in its creation – Herzog & de Meuron, Günther Vogt, Jasper Morrison and Ian Cartlidge – and independent voices that might explore the context for a new urban museum at the start of the twenty-first century – Oliver Wainwright, Wouter Davidts and Beatriz Colomina. Traditionally, books of this kind present the building before its opening, pristine and waiting to be sullied by users. For Tate Modern, however, we knew that the building had to be shown in use by those for whom it was designed. We have been fortunate to have James Morris as photographer, Nicola Bion as editor, and Peter Willberg as designer of a book that is the product of his customary flair and attention to detail. The publication of this book would not have been possible without the generosity of a group of committed friends of Tate, in particular Bernard Huppert, Mr and Mrs Michael Ringier, Uli and Rita Sigg, and Vitra Design Foundation, to whom we remain deeply grateful.

The west end of the Boiler House with St Paul's Cathedral in the distance.

Bankside, looking north
from Great Guildford Street
and Sumner Street, 1947.

Oliver Wainwright
Lofts and Caves

'The South Bank is notoriously ugly,' concluded the chairman of the public inquiry into Bankside power station in 1947, 'and even a large new industrial building could not seriously affect it.'[1] He was presiding over the fate of plans for the majestic brick fortress of electricity that would one day become Tate Modern. Such was the general opinion of the 'wrong side' of the Thames as late as the mid-twentieth century that a gargantuan oil-fired power plant could be built here in the middle of London, slap-bang opposite St Paul's Cathedral. After all, this temple of noxious fumes was only landing in an area deemed to be little more than an ugly jumble of wharves and warehouses, with their accompanying dens of Dickensian villainy.

Just seventy years later the stretch of the South Bank between Blackfriars and Southwark Bridge, where Bankside's chimney still stands sentinel, is almost unrecognisable. It has been transformed from a grubby dumping ground into one of the most desirable investment opportunities in the world, a magnet for international wealth from Singapore to Saudi Arabia. It has become a place where £20 million penthouses compete for attention at the top of teetering towers, a hotspot of supercharged property speculation where some of the tallest residential buildings in Europe are now rising from the ground.

It is an unlikely fate that has fulfilled the even more unlikely prediction of Bankside's original architect, Sir Giles Gilbert Scott. 'It has been said that the power station will dwarf St Paul's,' he told a press conference when his controversial design was unveiled in 1947 – before adding, in what seemed like a preposterous defence at the time, 'It will be more a question of the other buildings overshadowing the station than the station overshadowing them.'[2] With a pair of fifty-storey apartment towers arriving a stone's throw to the west, and the chamfered glass shafts of Richard Rogers' Neo Bankside development already looming behind Scott's brick shed, it seems that the architect's remarks were eerily prescient. And now, as if keeping up with the neighbours, Tate has sprouted a new tower of its own.

A twisted brick pyramid, chopped off before it has reached its pointed summit, it is a tower unlike any of the others. Its sharply faceted flanks erupt from the ground with a geological force, as if the building could be the product of a rupture along the South Bank's fault line. It has a primal heft, standing as a great brown cliff-face of baked clay from which the power station might once have been hewn. With its sheer sloping walls and monolithic mass, it recalls the monumental fortified structures of another age, channelling the power of the ancient Ziggurat of Ur and recalling the tapered mud brick towers of the walled city of Shibam in Yemen. The defensive air is magnified by the fact that its facade is only punctured by thin arrow-slit windows, giving it the look of a medieval siege tower, poised

to wage war across the Thames. And it's not hard to see why it was nicknamed the 'Dalek' when its menacing concrete frame first appeared on the skyline. Could it be Tate's new gun turret, here to safeguard the citadel of art and stop the army of property developers from encroaching any further?

• • •

The arresting brick bastion is the work of Herzog & de Meuron, the architects who first brought their minimal magic to Tate Modern in 2000, when they breathed new life into Gilbert Scott's mouldering brick shell with an unparalleled lightness of touch. It was an unlikely home for a new gallery of modern art: a brooding 1950s hulk, off-limits since its closure in the 1980s and surrounded by barbed wire-topped walls and defensive earthworks. And it was an even more unlikely choice of architect. The then unknown Swiss firm had built little more than a railway signal box and some offices in its home town of Basel, along with a small gallery pavilion in a garden in suburban Munich (the Goetz Collection).

Their entry to the 1994 competition to transform Bankside power station stood out for the simple reason that it proposed to do the least to the existing building. Others had grander plans. David Chipperfield proposed to lop off the chimney and insert a city-like plan of streets beneath a big glass roof. Tadao Ando wanted to skewer the power station with two vast glazed bars that would be dramatically cantilevered out over the riverside. Renzo

Piano saw his chance to build a Pompidou Centre mark II, filling the Turbine Hall with a stack of gallery floors, covered by a new high-tech roof. In Herzog & de Meuron's entry, however, it was quite hard to tell what they were even proposing to change.

The genius of their approach was that they knew when to stop. They realised that the role of the architect was not to drown out the power of the existing building, but to amplify the potential of what was already there. As Nicholas Serota, director of Tate since 1988, who had the foresight to choose the unlikely Bankside site in the mid-1990s, puts it: 'Whereas some of the other competition entries set out to mask the box or deal with perceived inadequacies of the box, Herzog & de Meuron saw that one simply had to twist it in a way that realised its potential.'[3]

Sitting in their studio in Basel, a cloistered complex that looks out on the Rhine in the centre of town, Jacques Herzog and Pierre de Meuron now preside over an empire very different to the small outfit they had sixteen years ago. In the time between the two Tate Modern projects, the partnership has grown to become one of the most sought-after firms of art museum architects in the world, completing projects from the de Young Museum in San Francisco (2005), to the Walker Art Center in Minneapolis (2005), the Parrish Art Museum in New York state (2012) and the Pérez Art Museum in Miami (2013) – a body of work for which they have won every accolade going, including the Pritzker Prize (2001) and the RIBA Royal Gold Medal (2007).

Today, in a rambling series of buildings across the courtyard from the partners' studio, 350 people are busily working away on everything from a gigantic museum of Asian art and design in Hong Kong, known as M+, to a new brick colosseum of football for Chelsea Football Club. But it is the revival of London's big brick shed that still they remember most fondly, as the project that catapulted them to global fame.

'I think the Turbine Hall is perhaps our best contribution,' says Jacques Herzog. 'And we didn't do so much. We stripped bare, made it much more of what it already was.' He describes the approach they took in the first phase as being the architectural equivalent of aikido, the Japanese martial art that turns the force of the enemy back on to himself. 'We didn't want to work against the building,' he says. 'It was really a monster, a great big mountain. We felt almost powerless in the face of it. Our approach was not based on a moral position, or a conservative idea of conservation, but it simply came from the sheer physical presence of the thing.'[4] The spatial power of the building was already latent in the majestic scale and proportions of Scott's brick box and the fine bones of the engineer's steelwork. It just had to be revealed.

The architects' most important move was doing away with the existing floor deck at ground level, thereby revealing the gaping chasm of the Turbine Hall in its full glory, and providing a momentous entrance sequence via a new ramp from the west, as if descending into some pharaoh's tomb. It is a colossal volume of a scale that could never be justified in a brand new building, supplying for free the iconic gesture expected of a modern gallery. Liberated from the obligation to create a signature shape, the architects' energies could be deployed elsewhere: in the subtle sequencing of gallery spaces with their changing ceiling heights; in the vertical procession of escalators between the floors; in the framing of views through Scott's cathedral windows out to the city, and back, through projecting glazed pods, into the Turbine Hall.

Nevertheless, as any aikido master knows, the fundamental aim is to knock the opponent off balance, and the project is at its most powerful where it dislodges the stability of Scott's stately pile. An entire corner of the building was sliced away at ground level (a trick the architects would later deploy even more dramatically at the CaixaForum in Madrid), where the café looks out on to the river, leaving the massive brick wall miraculously floating above. In one move, it reveals the fragility of what is not a load-bearing wall at all, but just a paper-thin brick cladding over a steel frame – a principle that, we will see, has been elevated into an elaborate game in the Switch House. Similarly, the two-storey glass 'light beam' on the roof of the power station stops short of reaching the eastern end of the building in order to undermine the apparently rigorous symmetry of Scott's building. 'We are not classicists,' says Herzog. 'We're not scared of symmetry, but we are not ideologically in favour of it. We like to start with the obvious, often symmetrical, form and then make arguments against it.'

Tate Modern, take one, was thus the ordinary made extraordinary: a series of subtle moves that reveal the inherent strangeness of putting art inside a power station. Fifteen years on, the strangeness has been cranked up a notch, with the arrival of one of the most enigmatic buildings that London has ever seen.

• • •

In their first Tate Modern project, Herzog & de Meuron played subtle games with Gilbert Scott's stately brick shed – here, for example, slicing away the entire north-western corner of the building, where the café is located, leaving the brick wall miraculously floating above.

If the first Tate Modern, now known as the Boiler House, had something of a didactic aim – designed to reveal and expose the true nature of Scott's great shed – then the new extension, named the Switch House, does its hardest not to give anything away at all. It is a building whose complex riddles and structural contortions are not easily solved.

What appears to be a blank, obliquely sculpted block from a distance tells little more on closer inspection. Visitors approaching from the west, towards the gallery's Main entrance, are greeted with a sheer brick cliff-face and a loading bay, and left with little choice but to proceed down the ramp into the gaping belly of the power station's turbine hall. Entering this epic void only exaggerates what comes next. There is now the choice of turning left, up the procession of escalators to the gallery levels, or turning right into the labyrinthine underworld that lurks beneath the twisted brick mountain.

It is here, in this Stygian realm of raw concrete and inky cast iron, that visitors discover the power station's former oil tanks, a clover-leaf of three buried concrete cylinders, big enough (and fortified enough) to hold the fuel that once powered a substantial chunk of London. Now drained and repurposed as spaces for performance, installation and film, they have been largely left as found. They exude the robust confidence of structures once made for a serious functional purpose, simply revealed and stripped back in a process of industrial archaeology.

Except that, in the hands of the maturer Herzog & de Meuron, it is no longer quite so straightforward. This subterranean level is punctuated by an irregular grid of pre-existing columns, giving it the air of a Roman hypocaust, disrupted by great buttress-like shafts of concrete that thrust through the space at a wayward slant. They are the structural fingers of the ziggurat above, skewering the basement on their way to find bedrock. The floor also slopes to and fro in unexpected planes, while a great tongue of silky smooth concrete licks down from the ceiling, forming a sweeping staircase that beckons you upwards into the light.

While in the first phase Herzog & de Meuron made a clear distinction between the hand of Scott and their own, here it is no longer obvious what previously existed and what has been introduced. The boundary between uncovering and intervening has become unsettlingly blurred. It is the first sign that whatever awaits upstairs will be a much stranger place than the Tate Modern you think you know.

• • •

The compelling strangeness of the Switch House is a result of the heady cocktail of forces that spawned the £260 million expansion to begin with. The building is a physical product of the gallery's success – and of the effect that success has had on both the surrounding area and the institution itself.

On the day that Tate Modern first opened to the public in May 2000, a staggering 35,000 people flooded through its doors. The crowds swelled to 1 million in the first six weeks and reached 5.3 million by the end of the year, exceeding projected visitor numbers almost three times over. First year luck, perhaps: the country was swept up in the thrill of the millennium and the chance to gawp inside this spectacular industrial cathedral of art. The popularity would surely never last.

But people came back. Again and again. By 2005 Tate Modern was receiving a steady 4 million visitors every year – compared to the 2.6 million of MoMA in New York and 2.5 million of the Pompidou Centre in Paris. While many of the UK's other flashy Millennium Projects languished – the £789 million Millennium Dome was almost pushed to bankruptcy and the £50 million Earth Centre in Doncaster was forced into administration – the £135 million refurbishment of an old power station soon became one of the most popular visitor attractions in the country. Herds of tourists were merrily helped across the Thames by the lean 'blade of light' of Norman Foster's new Millennium Bridge, whose famous wobble only added to its charm in the public's eyes, almost compensating for the clumsy way it lands in an awkward switchback in front of Tate.

With the seething crowds came the inevitable criticism that the gallery had become a victim of its own success. 'On some days it feels a little too much like Brent Cross or Lakeside,' wrote critic Jonathan Glancey in 2003, 'a shopping mall with busy cafés and

The Stygian realm of the former
oil tanks – an atmospheric world
punctuated by a grid of pre-existing
columns and the tilting buttress-like
shafts of the new Switch House
above, skewering the basement
on their way to find bedrock.

queues for the lavatories, only with a pretty good art collection.'[5] Three years later he described the building as a cross between a brutalist mall and the Seven Circles of Hell, raging that 'the galleries are often little more, for all their lofty grandeur, than corridors for crowds to tramp through in search of novelty, rarely stopping to look at the art on display.'[6] Author Will Self has compared the experience of traipsing through the crowded galleries to wheeling about amongst a herd of 'aesthetically crazed musk oxen'.[7]

An extension had been on the cards since day one, but it quickly became clear that the extra capacity would be needed sooner rather than later. And the sense of urgency was magnified by the unexpected and somewhat alarming effect that Tate was already having on its own surroundings.

The first signs of a very different Bankside came within a year of the gallery's opening, in the form of a proposal for a 32-storey tower of luxury flats right next to the top of Tate Modern's entrance ramp, on the site of an old printworks. A curved glass shaft crowned with a gleaming spire, it looked like something that had sailed in from the shores of Dubai. It was fiercely opposed by local residents and Tate, Nicholas Serota describing it as 'an opportunistic attempt to cash in for private gain on the public benefits that have been created' by the opening of the gallery.[8] It was refused by Southwark's planning committee, but granted

permission by the Mayor at appeal, before finally being quashed after a five-year battle. It would not be the last of such steroidal proposals; a precedent had been set.

Keen to pre-empt what might happen immediately behind it, Tate commissioned an urban study from the Richard Rogers Partnership in 2001 to examine what a potential extension, combined with a mixed-use public-private development, might look like. The results didn't bode particularly well. The images depict a big roof connecting the gallery to a commercial office building across a new piazza, along with what looks like a sliver of the Pompidou Centre grafted on to the power station's backside. As critic Rowan Moore wrote in the *Evening Standard* at the time, 'it shows every tic and commonplace of every precinct, plaza and mall everywhere from Plymouth to Gateshead at any time from the 1940s to now.' He warned that the result could end up turning the gallery into 'an echoing temple to art of uncertain usefulness, ringed with retail.'[9]

Thankfully the project never happened. Yet it was admirable that Tate should have had the foresight to take an interest in its wider neighbourhood, and indeed unusual that a museum should think to take on the role of urban planner at all. Fred Manson, who was Director of Regeneration at Southwark from 1994–2001, recalls that the arrival of the gallery was a phenomenal catalyst for improving the surrounding area: 'As soon as the Tate decided to come here, we said we had to raise the quality of our public realm to that of central London. This area had never been designed for visitors, but we had to make it feel as good as Westminster.'[10] With funding from central government, through the Cross River Partnership, Southwark embarked on an ambitious programme of improvements, commissioning a host of young architects to work on signage strategies and paving, as well as little squares and pocket parks.

The area around the power station soon began to change. The sites immediately to the south of Tate Modern were developed by Land Securities, in the form of three speculative office blocks designed by Allies and Morrison containing over one million square feet of commercial space. The site to the southwest would eventually be taken on by Richard Rogers in the form of Neo Bankside, a complex of 217 luxury flats developed by Grosvenor and Native Land, whose affordable housing component was provided off-site in cheaper parts of the borough. In Manson's eyes, it was inevitable that people would be priced out. 'Artists came to me and said we should be doing something to protect low rents in the area,' he says. 'I told them that I wasn't in the business of protecting low rents. I said they should become better artists so they could afford higher rents. Wherever art and artists move, development follows.'[11]

This supercharged process of gentrification, however, posed a serious danger to the future of Tate. The effect that the gallery was having on Bankside was threatening to stymie its own prospects for expansion. 'It soon became clear that, no matter what, there were going to be some really substantial buildings arriving right next door,' says Serota. 'We realised that if all this development went ahead, we would be really vulnerable in terms of what we could do on this site, because all these people would oppose us doing anything of any scale.'[12] The gallery had to get a foot in the door before it was swamped by the sky-high dreams of speculative investors, eager to profit from the cultural cachet that Tate itself had brought to the area.

The other trigger for expansion, says Serota, was internal. 'When we first took on the power station, we had one prime responsibility: to show the collection that had been built over the previous 85 years, together with a programme of exhibitions. But in thinking

about the next phase, we were aware that art itself was changing.'[13] An increasingly large proportion of Tate's acquisitions was made up of installation and site-specific sculpture, along with film, photography, sound and performance work. The mercurial world of new media didn't always sit happily in nice white boxes. 'We needed to stretch to being more environmental,' says Serota, 'providing big spaces for artists to work in performance and installation, but also more intimate spaces. That variety was key.'

• • •

An early document of ideas for Tate's future expansion, produced by Herzog & de Meuron in 2004, gives a hint of what that variety that Serota recognised as so important might be. It depicts a simple diagram of the existing Tate Modern, labelled 'Enfilade & Turbine Hall', then a '+' sign, then images of two other Herzog & de Meuron projects – the Schaulager in Basel, a gallery designed to feel like a refined Big Box storage warehouse, and the Kramlich Residence and Collection, a project that includes a contorted subterranean home for a media art collection in Napa Valley – labelled with the words 'Lofts & Caves'.

As you clamber up through the concrete helter-skelter of the new Switch House today, the legacy of these first thoughts is tangible. Indeed, the spatial variety is the first thing that strikes you. The building takes visitors on a journey from the underworld of the Tanks, up along a twisting, turning promenade that leads to some galleries of a voluminous warehouse scale, and others of intimate dimensions, some arranged as a classical enfilade, others carved out like little concrete caves beneath the stairs.

'We think it is very important to have this variety of experiences,' says Pierre de Meuron. 'When you are in the galleries, you look at the wall, the floor, the art. If you spend half a day or a day at the Tate you need something else. It's a small city, so it needs these different spaces to function.'

The primary new galleries, which expand the exhibition space by around sixty per cent, have been cleverly fitted into the orthogonal volume of what was the old switch house, between the Turbine Hall and the new brick ziggurat, where until recently electrical transformers still whirred. Power company EDF consolidated its operations to the southeastern corner of the building in 2007, allowing the western end to be freed up for what is now three generous floors of exhibition space. They are arranged in line with the existing gallery levels in the Boiler House and fitted with the same rough sawn oak floors. 'They should feel like an organic continuation of the museum,' explains Herzog.[14]

Step out from the galleries into the expressive spaces of the brick and concrete pyramid, however, and it feels like entering an entirely different world. The exposed ribs of the building's structural concrete cage soar up between the floors, through a vertiginous triple height void, with the dramatic force of a Piranesian perspective. Leaning through the full height of the building like mighty medieval buttresses, they create a sense of inevitable vertical movement, an impression enhanced by subtle slopes in the floors, which

The Switch House staircase is one of the most elaborate Herzog & de Meuron have ever designed, leading visitors on a vertical promenade of sweeping spirals and twisting dog-legs, with places to sit and loiter along the way.

Sequence of study models
(from left to right):
Level 0–1 Tanks stairs
Level 1–2 stairs
Level 2–4 art stairs
Level 4–10 tower stairs.

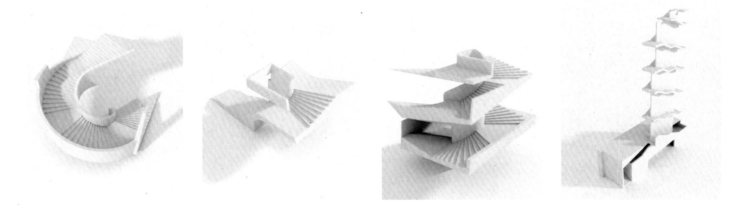

ramp incessantly upwards, making walking between the different levels feel like traversing a continuous topography.

'The slope is barely perceptible,' says Project Director John O'Mara, Associate of Herzog & de Meuron. 'But it's there to emphasise the progression through the space as you're hiking up through the building, driving you towards the stairs that pinwheel around the floors.'[15] The staircase, ever a preoccupation of Herzog & de Meuron, is one of their most elaborate yet. It begins life in the basement as a grand sweeping spiral, tapering out as it spills on to level 1, before moving to the pinched southeastern corner of the site, where it rises in a dog-leg to level 2. It picks up again in the opposite corner, spiralling in a generous cascade for two more levels, past full height windows looking into the staff offices – 'so that visitors are aware that there's a brain behind what they're seeing,' says Serota.[16]

Throughout this journey, there are frequent places to pause and linger. As the building's geometry twists to and fro, the concrete structure distorts, creating areas to perch or lean in the depth of the columns and beams. The deformations create a landscape of enticing nooks and niches, incidental leftover spaces to loiter in, encouraged in places by rudimentary plywood seating – a nod to the wooden shuttering in which the concrete was cast.

'We really wanted it to feel like the kind of spaces you find in nature, where you sit under a tree or on a rock,' says Herzog, 'spaces that are more inviting, where you can just sit and be yourself. It's a bit like in a cathedral, with these wonderful smaller areas where you can be in a more intimate condition, but feel part of a bigger whole.'[17]

The generosity of all this space for circulation is in part a response to the results of a survey undertaken during the development of the brief, which found that one of the main reasons people gave for visiting Tate Modern was to encounter other people. The building's role, beyond the display of art, was to provide a mixing chamber for people-watching and incidental meeting. It is an approach that has also informed the nature of the

new educational spaces. Level 5, above the gallery floors, is devoted to Tate Exchange, an initiative that Serota describes as 'a combination of the Open University, art school, TED Talks, and *Guardian* debates, all wrapped into one.'[18] Sessions will take a drop-in format, no doubt helped by the loose-fit, free-flowing nature of the building itself.

This looping, switchback flow of spaces creates a meandering pace, forcing visitors to slow down as they wander up the foothills of the mountain. But as the building rises and breaks free from the Boiler House, things begin to change. What feels like a languid horizontal landscape on the lower levels transforms into an emphatically vertical sequence as the Switch House shoots for the skies. From level 4 onwards, the staircase narrows to half its width, pulled into the central concrete core of the tower where it runs back and forth for the remaining six floors, marching at a brisker pace as it advances towards the summit.

As you ascend through the upper levels, past a studio floor, staff offices, a dedicated members' floor and a restaurant, to the public terrace and bar, where you might expect the building to dissolve into the clouds, the opposite thing happens. Whereas most structures get progressively thinner and lighter as they rise, due to the need to support less mass, the tapering geometry of the Switch House means that the cage of columns and beams becomes ever more dense. Just when you would expect the hefty concrete grid to fade into a gossamer crown, it is more present than ever, converging in a contorted knot at the top of the building, where spectacular views of London's skyline are framed by the muscular enclosure.

It is a counterintuitive perversion that provides an apt climax at the summit of this tortured Tower of Babel, a building that defies all logical rules of construction – where the brick facade hangs like folded fabric and some of the seemingly load-bearing columns don't actually meet their slabs. Only about half of the concrete cage at the top actually serves a structural purpose.

• • •

Exactly why and how this architecture was formed can only be explained by unpicking its origins – which currently reside on the southern side of Basel, across the railway tracks from the historic centre, in a building just as enigmatic as Tate Modern's Switch House.

In the industrial zone of Dreispitz, amongst a jumble of warehouses, stands an odd concrete tower which looks a bit like an apartment block caught halfway through demolition from the ground up. A blank concrete core rises to a point midway up the building, where a facade of domestic life is cantilevered out on angled props in the manner of a medieval fortification.

Inside stand row upon row of vitrines containing shelves stacked full of intriguing alien objects. There are globules of melted glass and mounds of expanded foam,

crumpled sheets of metal along with blocks of plaster, resin and concrete that have been cast, moulded, bubbled and baked in a beguiling process of material alchemy. It feels like walking into a natural history museum of the future, where new species of form and matter have been subjected to an accelerated process of evolution.

This *Wunderkammer* of odds and ends comprises the Herzog & de Meuron archives as part of the newly established Jacques Herzog and Pierre de Meuron Kabinett (Foundation). The Kabinett contains the meticulously catalogued output of the office since Jacques and Pierre began working together in 1978, along with a collection of artworks assembled from a now illustrious list of artist friends over the decades. A wall-sized photograph by Hiroshi Sugimoto hangs in a space on the ground floor opposite a Dan Graham maquette. Elsewhere there are pieces by Ai Weiwei, with whom they designed Beijing's 'Bird's Nest' Olympic stadium (2008), and a photograph by Thomas Ruff, with whom they collaborated on the concrete facade of their library in Eberswalde, Germany (1999). It is hard to think of a pair of architects more steeped in the art world, or with a greater sensitivity to how artists like their work to be shown.

Upstairs several vitrines are dedicated to tapering pyramidal blocks in various stages of evolution. There are some carved from blue styrofoam, others formed in crystalline perspex, and still more made from wiry cages, like deformed lobster pots. Some

appear to be trios of cylindrical grain silos converging into a pointed wigwam, others look more like wonky heaps of Lego bricks. They all have one thing in common: these are the embryonic experiments for what would become the Switch House.

'We have often tried out stupid things,' says Herzog. 'You never know where it will go, but sometimes it leads to unexpected results.'[19] Tate Modern's extension was one such unexpected result, as a project that started out life as a very different kind of building. The design that received planning permission in 2007 took the form of a glacial mountain of cast glass blocks, stacked up behind the former power station like a teetering pile of ice cubes. The tapering form was defined by the maximum envelope allowed by neighbours' rights of light and protected views of St Paul's (a jelly-mould that the built Switch House also fits within), while the cubes effectively represented the different parts of the museum programme, arranged in a vertical stack.

It was a startling proposal that was partly a product of Tate's lingering desire to prove itself. 'There was a certain amount of self-imposed pressure to answer some of the criticisms that had been made a decade earlier when we took on the power station,' explains Serota, 'principally that we didn't have the conviction to do a totally new building.'[20]

The Switch House taking shape, June 2014. During its construction, when the tapering concrete frame first became visible on the skyline, the building was nicknamed the Dalek.

The result trumpeted a klaxon call of newness that, while it thrilled potential donors, was met with vocal dismay by the heritage lobby. Gavin Stamp, an architectural historian and biographer of Giles Gilbert Scott, said the glass cluster was 'not only pretentious, excessively domineering and ill thought out in itself', but that it would 'gravely damage Scott's building both physically and aesthetically'.[21] It was a view with which Herzog & de Meuron now seem inclined to agree.

'It would have been a *nightmare*,' says Herzog, 'It was just too alien, too far away from the existing building.'[22] The change of heart, which came about after fundraising was delayed by the recession, was driven by a dawning realisation that the surrounding context of Bankside would soon be one of expressive glass towers. To stand out, they would do better to turn the volume down and go back to brick.

But it wasn't to be any kind of brick. The architects decided to take the constructional logic of the power station – a structural frame clad with a brick skin – and propel it to the next extreme. The structure would be a mighty mineral frame, a muscular cage grown from the massive concrete-walled Tanks and wrenched into shape by the planning restrictions. The brick skin would be as light as a textile, a perforated screen of blocks hung like chainmail

over the concrete skeleton. It would be a continuous shroud, giving the impression that the building was a sheer impenetrable block.

'Ideally we would have liked no windows,' says Herzog. 'Windows are difficult. A simple form always looks best without.' The architects have long tried to evade the window by designing facades of perforated mesh that give the illusion of a solid mass, while allowing light in and views out. It has always been a tricky balance to strike. At the de Young Museum in San Francisco, which features a similarly twisted tower wrapped with perforated metal mesh, the architects again wanted to keep the sense of a monolithic block, but were convinced to slice open a long letterbox viewing window. 'The client was right,' concedes Herzog. 'He said if it was an observation tower, then people would want to have a clear view and not always be hidden behind a screen.' It was a lesson they sadly forgot a few years later at the CaixaForum in Madrid (2008) where, by the time visitors have reached the restaurant at the summit of the museum, the view out over the city's rooftops is obscured by a mostly opaque veil of cor-ten steel. 'I admit that's a mistake,' says Herzog. 'We were scared of destroying the form. I wish we could somehow punch a hole in it. We are quite experienced now, but we still don't trust ourselves sometimes.'[23]

The brick facade is hung like chainmail over the concrete frame, providing an ever-changing projection of dappled light across the floors and walls, with views framed by the combination of the thick concrete grid and brick blinkers drawn like a blind across the windows.

      The facade of Tate Modern's Switch House treads a fine line between solid wall and diaphanous veil, with not always happy results. From the outside, the effect of the form as a monolithic chiselled rock is reduced by the number of horizontal openings seemingly slashed at random across the facade. From the inside, the experience can be frustrating, when particular views are obscured by the ever-present chequerboard of bricks. Yet, in other places, the effect is mesmerising, where the screen casts an ever-changing projection of dappled light across the floors and walls, and where views are specifically framed by the combination of the thick concrete grid and brick blinkers drawn like a blind across the windows.

      It is just another one of the unexpected, illogical and utterly beguiling features of this consistently challenging building, a twisted tower whose contortions are a manifestation of the invisible forces shaping the city, the art and the institution, but whose enigmas will never quite be decoded – perhaps just like the work it contains.

Gerhard Richter's letter to Nicholas
Serota, 8 March 1994: his response
to the Tate Gallery of Modern Art
Questionnaire, 5 January 1994.

Gerhard Richter · Bismarckstraße 50 · 50672 Köln · Telefon 0221-525353 · Fax -519694

Tate Gallery
Mr. Nicholas Serota
Millbank

GB LONDON SW1P 4RG

March 8, 1994

Dear Nicholas,

I' m sorry for my delay in answering your letter, and I' m
more sorry for my incapacity in answering your questions.
This is embarrassing for me, because I' m interested in
architecture, but that matter is so diffictult for me and
my aversion to architects is so distinct, that I rather
could try to design a museum than being able to give you
any useful answer.

So I only can wish you good luck and all best for this great
and exciting project of a New Tate.

Sincerely yours,

Wouter Davidts
A Ziggurat of Brick and Concrete

MUSEUM…
On joue ici jusqu'à la fin du monde.
Marcel Broodthaers[1]

What finally turned out to be so simple was quite difficult
to achieve at the beginning.
Herzog & de Meuron[2]

In January 1994, when the project for a new building for the collection of modern art for the Tate Gallery at Bankside was underway, a questionnaire was sent to artists worldwide. Determined to take the experiences and opinions of living artists into account in the development of a new museum building, Tate officials invited a long list of British and international artists to disclose which museums or galleries served as their favourite exhibition venues, which recent projects they considered a success, and what could be regarded as 'the most common mistake made in recent museum architecture'.[3] Whereas the majority of the artists that responded to the personal invitation listed both their preferred and least-liked museum buildings, German artist Gerhard Richter apologised in a letter to Tate Director Nicholas Serota for his 'incapacity in answering [his] questions'. Even though he expressed his sincere interest in architecture, he declared that the matter was too difficult for him: 'my aversion for architects is so distinct, that I rather could try to design a museum than being able to give you any useful answer.'[4]

Richter's declaration is remarkable yet not unique. Although the exchange between art and architecture has served as a primary locus of cultural production for some decades, the relationship between artists and architects generally remains lukewarm. Despite the frequency and intensity of exchange, the encounter between art and architecture is Janus-faced. Whereas some artists and architects have entered into fruitful collaborations, others continue to cherish an adversarial competition.[5] The architectural extravaganza displayed in the many new museum buildings erected in the past five decades undoubtedly fuelled the antagonism. As early as 1979, the Belgian architecture critic Geert Bekaert observed that the museum appeared to be the exemplary building type in which architecture seized its assignment – the housing of art – as a mere alibi for self-realisation.[6] Rightfully artists voiced their indignation about the architects' lack of restraint in museum design and their misplaced desire for expression – tellingly, Hans Hollein hand-signed the Museum Abteiberg, Mönchengladbach in 1982. 'These buildings', the American artist Donald Judd declared in 1991, 'make a joke of architecture, of art, of culture, of the community, and of the whole society.'[7] In her response to Tate's questionnaire in 1994, British artist Rachel Whiteread mockingly

replied that the most common mistake made in new museum design was that 'architects often forget that art has to be shown in them'.[8] In a recent interview on the 'Museum of the Future', artist John Baldessari suggested a practical solution to the conceited stance of architects: 'You could have their building, and next to them another, a simple box to show the art.'[9]

The Basel-based architects Herzog & de Meuron started their practice in 1978, the year following the opening of the Centre Pompidou in Paris and the start of what has broadly been recognised as the museum boom. From the very beginning, however, the young architects struck a different position. Rather than joining the fiercely antagonistic battle between art and architecture, they opted for a sincere dialogue. Instead of seeing artists as adversaries, they made them allies, as they noted in 1994, for their own interest in 'learning what architecture is, in finding out about today's possibilities for architecture and urbanism, in what these disciplines can contribute to every life, to everyone's life'.[10] Even more, they experienced art as an imaginative realm, counter to the often self-directed and rather defensive stance of architecture. From early on, they engaged in what they experienced as 'natural' alliances with artists, resulting in collaborative projects with such now prominent artists as Rémy Zaugg, Olafur Eliasson, Pipilotti Rist, Rosemarie Trockel, Ai Weiwei, and even Richter himself.[11]

Invariably one wonders whether the architects' close acquaintance with artists is the foundation for their present-day success and approval in the art and museum

world. At the time of writing, Herzog & de Meuron have built no fewer than fifteen museums on almost all continents, thirteen of which are public and two private, while another nine projects are in the final design stages or in the process of being built. In contrast to some of their colleagues, the portfolio of museum projects by Herzog & de Meuron is strikingly diverse in terms of institutional programme and geographical location, as well as in material appearance and spatial organisation. Projects such as the Goetz Collection (1989–92), a small gallery for a private collection in Munich that received international acclaim, London's Tate Modern (1995–2000), the conversion of the former Bankside Power Station that benchmarked their arguably rather late arrival on the international stage of museum architecture, the most recently opened Parrish Art Museum in Water Mill, New York State (2009–12) and the Pérez Art Museum in Miami (2006–13) are admittedly very different buildings. Their design for the new extension of Tate Modern once again strikes a different note.

Whereas some of their colleagues have clearly opted for a signature style or a recurring formal vocabulary that allows one to attribute buildings to the respective designer, Herzog & de Meuron sanction diversity and distinction. The specific character of each project is the product of the architects' relentless determination to come up with a subjective interpretation of the brief, as well as formulate a particular response to the individual context. Every new commission and situation demands a specific approach and a novel formulation. As early as 1994, the architects conveyed that 'the making of architecture, its so-called design, is intimately related to the perception of the world'. Architecture is more than just a problem-solving imposition or functional reorganisation of the world, it is a rich means to make sense of that very world. 'Architecture,' they contended, 'is like an instrument of perception.'[12]

Herzog & de Meuron's profoundly humanistic formulation of the role and meaning of both the practice and the object of architecture strongly rhymes with the institutional project of the art museum. In the museum we encounter both objects and images that have a vested interest in our very perception of the world by questioning, reconfiguring or rearticulating it, visually, materially and conceptually. Contemporary society is no longer static or slowly evolving but almost completely commercialised, fleeting and media-saturated. In this state of affairs, art remains one of the few remaining spheres in contemporary culture where, with a certain slowness and freedom, one can work on those meanings and ideas that constitute civil society and social exchange. An artwork could, after the wonderful eponymous poem by Jorge Luis Borges, serve as 'a compass'. It potentially provides guidance in our continuous attempts to understand the 'infinite babble that is, per se, the history of the world'. In that 'hodgepodge', Borges writes, 'both Rome and Carthage, he and you and I, my life that I don't grasp, this painful load of being riddle, randomness, or code and all of Babel's gibberish stream by.'[13] Artworks don't provide answers, merely directions. As obdurate as they often can be, they offer possibilities to readjust our perception of the world and subsequently to recalibrate our understanding. 'You can learn how to make good decisions from art,' Chris Dercon, then Tate Modern Director, advocated, 'and the museum can show you the way.'[14] Indeed, the museum is the place *par excellence* to accommodate and host the conversation that art inevitably entails and provokes, and it does so in public view. It collects, shows and shares with its visitors the abundant produce of the relentless work done in art and by artists.

When invited to participate in the architecture competition in late 1994, Herzog & de Meuron tackled the commission with their characteristic sensitivity and precision. They listened to Tate's explicit demand to avoid an architectural *prima donna* or signature building, as the museum wanted to suit the needs and desires of contemporary art and artists by means of a building with 'sufficient patina ... for the art to be comfortable rather than simply on show'.[15] Instead of succumbing to the temptation to design an extravagant showcase for their own creative talent rather than for the display of art, the architects tried to deliver a radical antidote to what Donald Judd once termed 'the prevailing regurgitated art and architecture'.[16] They did not opt for a dialectical confrontation between the old and the new, but adhered to an approach that they described as 'closer to Viollet-le-Duc, with a pinch of Asian martial arts'. Rather than fully defying the building, they adopted 'the Aikido strategy of using the opponent's energy to gain the upper hand'.[17] Indeed, Herzog & de Meuron's entry for the first stage of the architectural competition in November 1994 displayed the intricate play with the original industrial structure that still marks the building today.

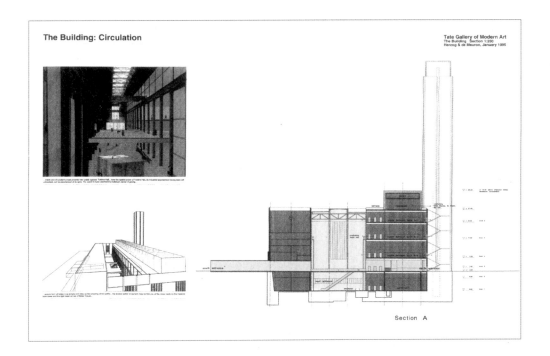

'The architectural concept for the conversion of the Power Station is radically simple, economical and almost self-evident', the architects wrote. 'It takes the maximum profit from the existing building structure. It really deals with the existing volume and with the existing materials.'[18] Herzog & de Meuron understood that the size of the original Bankside Power Station did not correspond with the scale of a traditional museum: the two naves of the building, the Boiler House and the Turbine Hall respectively, were too vast for a conventional art gallery. To grant the building a human scale that tallied with museum activity, they realised they had to insert within it a completely new building with adequate spaces, to 'invent' the building as a museum while keeping close to what was actually there.[19] Consequently their scheme safeguarded the original spatial zoning and massing of the building by densely filling the volume of the Boiler House with spaces of very different functions, forms and sizes, leaving the Turbine Hall open – a spectacular urban void. Of all the participating teams in the first stage of the competition, only Herzog & de Meuron sought to preserve the space of the Turbine Hall in its totality.[20] Their plan was to convert it into an urban foyer that would 'make the Tate Gallery of Modern Art a very lively and public space, one of London's most attractive covered public spaces'.[21] In their design for the second stage in January 1995, Herzog & de Meuron followed the same general line, advancing the Turbine Hall as the key feature of the project. The accompanying perspectival drawing of the Turbine Hall soon became the seminal image from the competition.[22] While it proficiently communicated the strategic simplicity of

Olafur Eliasson's *Weather Project*,
the 2003 commission in The Unilever
Series in the Turbine Hall,
October 2003 – March 2004.

the winning design, it above all conveyed the potentially fruitful encounter between art and architecture that indeed would later occur in the vast vestibule of the museum.

In many respects the success of Tate Modern surpassed all expectations. Not only did the museum welcome almost three times the number of visitors than initially calculated, these same visitors also warmly embraced both the institution and the building while visiting the collection displays, temporary exhibitions and, finally, the yearly artist's interventions in the Turbine Hall.[23] The institution emerged as one of the most prosperous projects in civic terms – unlike any other, the museum managed to draw in a public of different ages, distinct cultural upbringing and diverse ethnic backgrounds. The most surprising phenomenon, however, was the direct engagement, new modes of behaviour and unanticipated forms of commitment displayed by the visitors during their visits – exemplified by the astounding behaviour of the crowd in the Turbine Hall at the time of Olafur Eliasson's immensely popular *Weather Project* from October 2003 to March 2004, for which the artist transformed the space with a mirrored ceiling, a bright yellow artificial sun and puffs of steam.[24] While the regular overcrowding of the building fairly quickly stimulated a plan for the expansion of the museum, Tate realised that it was not going to solve the problem by providing more and larger spaces. It would also have to alter its mode of address.

In a first press release of July 2006 announcing the plans for 'Transforming Tate Modern. A New Museum for 21st Century Britain', the role and position of the public were given prime position, preceding contemporary art practice and the collection respectively. Indeed, fifteen years after the initial conception, Tate staff realised that 'the world has changed dramatically and the expectations of the Internet generation are much more sophisticated and demanding'. The growing call for active engagement with art, and contemporary art in particular, provided the main stimulus for the extension: 'Tate needs to respond to the increasing demand for its education programmes through the creation of new spaces and facilities.' Even though it was envisaged from the outset that Tate Modern would be realised in two phases, the unexpectedly intense life and novel use of the building forced the institution to proceed faster than expected in further developing the potential of the Bankside Power Station building and site. It is not surprising then, that the educational and social mandate of the museum prevailed in the new plans for its expansion, now achieving the same level of importance as the need to provide 'more space for new areas for contemporary art, particularly for new areas of contemporary visual culture including photography, film, video and performance' and the need to grant 'more space to show Tate's growing collection'.[25]

Significantly, this major shift translated into the 'Architectural Brief' for the extension that was drafted in 2007. The first sentence describes Tate Modern's further development as having 'the objective to create one of the most exciting new cultural buildings in the world, designed to show the full breadth of contemporary art in the 21st century', but this

is immediately followed by the statement that 'audience engagement and learning will form the heart of the new museum'.[26] This key place for social and educational exchange, however, does not signal a lesser importance for the artists or the artworks in the collection. 'Artists will play an important role in shaping the project and Tate will continue to develop one of the finest collections of contemporary art in the world,' the brief reassures. Yet, unlike in 1994, artists did not receive a questionnaire; instead the public did. In 2004 people were asked why they wanted to visit Tate, and what their experiences were. Instead of questioning the best possible conditions for art display, the institution wanted to learn about the motivations, attitudes, perceptions and reactions of visitors to Tate.[27]

A most astonishing outcome of the survey (confirmed by further research in 2010) was that less than a quarter of the visitors came for inspiration and aesthetic experience only. Many more came to obtain knowledge and to encounter people. This result obviously strengthened the museum's early chosen direction, and consequently informed the architectural brief and the ensuing design by Herzog & de Meuron. Whereas the initial scheme of Tate Modern was primarily driven by concerns about the display of artworks, the role and participation of the public became the decisive factor in the second phase of the project. As Chris Dercon later said, 'the museum no longer sees its ever-growing audiences as a hindrance.' Radically defying the common lambasting of populism, Tate Modern was going to embrace the public as never before: 'It will become a new type of public space, one for social play and innovation, facilitating new forms of art, creativity and thinking, where people will look at and interact with art as well as with each other. Learning will become an artistic activity in itself.'[28]

The decision to take seriously the educational and social mandate of the museum, I would argue, is fundamentally a progressive one.[29] Tate Modern's expanded site opens at a time when we are seeing seismic shifts in the contemporary art and museum world. The rising prices of artworks on the art market coincide with the shrinking budgets of public institutions in the Atlantic world. Private museums and foundations, often with greater wealth, resources and gaudier facilities, have come to dominate the scene with public institutions being squeezed in a rather uneven competition. In this state of affairs, expensive public buildings, Dercon recently admitted, might become a relic of social democracy's willingness to invest in art and culture: 'Probably the new Tate Modern is one of the last examples of this period.' Nevertheless, he argued, there were 'many good reasons and necessities' for building it, which stem directly from the major distinction between public and private institutions, namely the unwavering civic mandate of the former.[30] Apart from the long-term thinking and continuity, institutions like Tate Modern continue to promote the public exchange between art, artists and people. This communal mediation forms the very heart of public institutions, a responsibility that private institutions do not need to take on and, arguably, rarely do. A commonly expressed lament has been that the scholarly tenet of museums has to contend with a rapidly expanding social vocation of public education and popular leisure. Tate Modern apparently realised that the time was ripe to reverse the argument. Rather than mourning, it set out to explore to what extent it could exploit the development, precisely to distinguish itself from other institutions within the larger sphere of the art world. Yet this decision, Tate Modern recognised, would also have drastic consequences for the architectural brief. As Chris Dercon conceded, 'conceiving a perfect space for art and artists I don't think is a priority any longer.'[31]

It had always been Tate's intention to 'complete' Tate Modern by bringing into use the other parts of the Power Station, such as the Switch House and the oil tanks underneath it. However, it was only in 2007 that it became possible, when the electricity company that owns and operates the electricity substation on the site shrank its plant to the eastern part of the Switch House. As in the first phase, Herzog & de Meuron took the existing edifice and its morphology as the point of departure, using the clover-shaped form of the subterranean oil tanks. In one of the earliest schemes for the architecture competition in 1995, the architects had already signalled a potential future use of this dramatic underground structure, which could be 'converted into pavilions and playgrounds for children and adults'. Both literally and figuratively the oil tanks provided the very foundation upon which, and from which, the new building would arise. These truly as-found, industrial spaces, the architects wrote in a presentation sheaf for one of the early design schemes for the new extension in 2008, would constitute the kernel of the museum's future identity:

> *The oil tanks are not simply the physical foundation of the new building but also the starting point for intellectual and curatorial approaches which have changed to meet the needs of a contemporary museum at the beginning of the 21st century. These approaches require a range of gallery spaces both larger and smaller along with 'as found' spaces of less conventional shape.*[32]

However, the envelope for the rising concrete structure was not derived from the clover-shape of the oil tanks. The slightly sloping and warped exterior surface of the tower rising at the south side of the Power Station was generated by the existing brick building, visitor routing on the Southwark site and the zoning laws for light and views of St Paul's Cathedral. The consequence of this clash of two different geometries can be experienced in the passageway connecting the Turbine Hall with the Tanks. Reminiscent of the elementary volumes of the sculptor Ronald Bladen (1918–88), a diagonal line of inclined, massive concrete pillars pierces through the ceiling and disrupts both the orthogonal logic of the Switch House and the circular set-up of the oil tanks.

The area with these robust concrete columns is the only section of the museum where the confrontation between existing structure and the added architecture is openly disclosed, albeit in a very subtle fashion. Contrary to the common trend in museum expansion, Herzog & de Meuron consciously decided not to add a new, self-contained wing to the building, but to expand the existing site into a coherent whole.[33] The scheme does not play the different architectural parts against each other, but unites them while respecting their different spatial constitution and material quality. As in the first phase of the project, the architects' approach was to preserve the overall spatial diagram of the existing building, and distribute the new programme throughout the existing and newly created spaces. Rather than attempting to create a uniformity of space, Herzog & de Meuron opted for a sincere juxtaposition: 'This dialogue between the raw and the refined, the found and the new, lies at the heart of the architectural vision for the building.'[34] In dialogue with the curators, the architects made a clear division between those parts of the programme that would be situated in the oil tanks, in the newly added tower, and in the former volume of the Switch House respectively. This separation becomes plainly legible in the ground plan. Contemporary practices such as film, video, and performance are allocated primarily to the underground areas in the oil tanks, whereas the presentation of the collection and temporary exhibitions are assigned to well-proportioned and flexible gallery spaces located within the spatial confines of the Switch House – not unlike the neat insertion of the display galleries in the perimeter of the Boiler House on the other side of the Turbine Hall. The volume of the new tower primarily

Study model by Herzog & de Meuron
exploring the ideas of the 'ceremonial
route' in the Switch House.

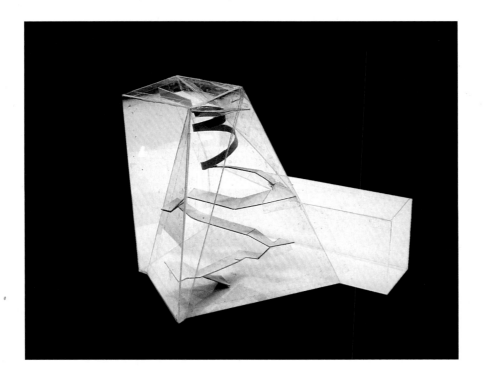

houses social and educational programmes, with an array of cafés, lounges, restaurants, shops, classrooms, studio spaces, member rooms and a spectacular viewing terrace distributed over ten floors, all of which are connected by a complex route of ramps and stairs – appropriately called 'the ceremonial route' by the architects. This *promenade* starts at underground level with a majestically curved staircase that is situated precisely on the virtual 'seam' between the existing building and the addition.

Tate Modern will possess a unique diversity of spaces, unequalled by any other museum in the world. In contrast to Yoshio Taniguchi, who turned the assorted buildings that make up the New York Museum of Modern Art into one seamless, spatial whole in 2004 – all the while promising even to make architecture disappear – Herzog & de Meuron articulated the different constituent parts of the building, while retaining a sense of coherence.[35] Here architecture neither disappears nor overbears, but manifests, confirms even, its structural role in instituting the space of the museum.

Ever since the advent of the Centre Pompidou, which made a radical break with the traditional appearance of the museum as a temple for the arts, museums of modern and contemporary art have acquired all kinds of shapes and appearances. Today museums resemble hospitals, prisons, jewel boxes, spacecraft, offices, boats and even fish. In contrast with the Centre Pompidou, however, few of these architectural oddities stem from

Robert Smithson
Mirrored Ziggurat, 1966.

Robert Smithson
Entropic Landscape, 1970.

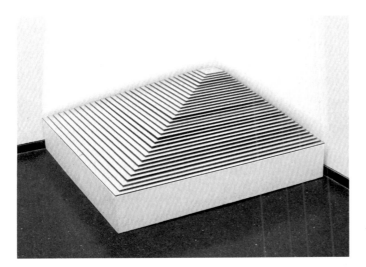

an internal aspiration for museological innovation. The architectural pyrotechnics first and foremost meet an external agenda to provide a city with a landmark, to mark the cityscape, to add value to the surrounding urban fabric and to stimulate urban renewal. While Herzog & de Meuron's addition to Tate Modern certainly yields to all of these latter factors, the design also delivers a sincere and intelligent response to some of the crucial developments in the art and museum world. In the combined force of its material constitution and spatial organisation, the scheme responds to the needs of the contemporary art museum today, while consciously holding back from explicit typological innovation.[36]

So far the recurring terms used to describe the tower are a tent, a pyramid, a mineral block and even the Tower of Babel. An architectural model made for an early design scheme held in the vast archives of Herzog & de Meuron in Basel, however, prompts another, highly noteworthy term.[37] Consisting of stacked glass plates of different outlines, the model gave shape to the awe-inspiring scheme of 2007 that consisted of a stack of boxes, clad in a surface made primarily of glass. Even though much more irregular in appearance, the model is reminiscent of the work *Mirrored Ziggurat* 1966 by Robert Smithson (1938–1973), constructed from diagonally receding mirror panes. Even though a singular sculpture, the two perpendicular sides indicate that the object is supposed to be supported by one, if not two, existing walls of a building – i.e. a corner – not unlike the towering addition to the Bankside Power Station. Closer scrutiny of the spatial organisation of Herzog & de Meuron's design gives the term 'ziggurat' further currency – not least when the glass facade was exchanged for a brick lattice in later design stages.

The brick mesh of Tate Modern's addition veils a stacking of levels around which a route spirally mounts to the top, not unlike the type of Assyrian or Babylonian

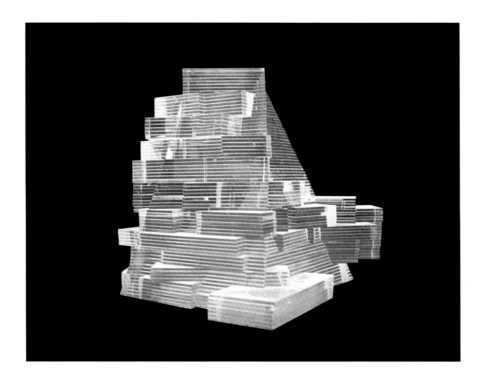

Temple-tower that was erected in the 3rd millennium BCE. Built in brick mud and often faced with baked brick, this Mesopotamian edifice took the form of a truncated pyramid built in diminishing stages, each level being reached by ramps. It is the building type that is supposed to have inspired the biblical story of the Tower of Babel and the ensuing rich tradition of its depiction in Western painting.[38] Yet the historical semblance is not limited to material shape and spatial outline. In his first eyewitness account of Etemenanki, the ziggurat at Babylon, the Greek historian Herodotus notes that 'about halfway up is a resting place, with seats for repose, where those who ascend sit down and rest'. His description of the 'great shrine … with a great and well-covered couch, and a golden table nearby' that were to be found on the top level, beautifully resonates with the area at the zenith of Tate Modern's tower, where the shrine and altar have been replaced by the secular function of a *belvedere* terrace with bar.[39]

Museums have been compared repeatedly to secular temples, where the truth of God and religion is replaced by the beauty and power of art. Yet the tower at Tate Modern is not intended as a place to venerate art in traditional terms, but rather first and foremost to 'establish ways of developing the public's visual literacy and understanding of Modern and Contemporary art'.[40] It constitutes the space where the institution intends to perform its role as 'sociable and sophisticated learning space that enables imaginative and alternative forms of study, research, debate, and teaching'.[41] Phrased differently, the tower is

Pieter Bruegel the Elder
The Tower of Babel c.1563
Oil paint on panel, 60 × 74.5 cm
Museum Boijmans Van Beuningen
Rotterdam.

that specific portion of the building where the museum hopes to transmute into a library of sorts. In doing so, the institution wilfully reassesses its etymological origin, the Ptolemaic *mouseion* at Alexandria founded in 300 BCE, which was first and foremost a study collection with library attached, a repository of knowledge, a place of scholars and philosophers and historians.[42] Tate Modern, however, proposes that the purpose of the museum is no longer the private privilege of scientists and specialists, but an activity shared and performed by the wider public. Seen in this light, Tate's ziggurat does not so much symbolise the fatality of the Babylonian confusion of tongues that inaugurates the historical process of globalisation, as the contemporary hope that the museum can mediate the very process that more and more determines our twenty-first-century society. Art has served for centuries as one of the key domains within which humans negotiate their existence by representing the world, in either figurative or abstract form. The modern invention of the institution of the museum has, however, provided a secular abode to assess the outcome relentlessly. The museum provides us with a place to study the images and objects produced by our artistic contemporaries. In this regard the museum rhymes with Borges's conception of the library. In his cryptic yet mesmerising essay *The Library of Babel* (1941), which one could read as a critical allegory of the museum of contemporary art, Borges describes the library as 'unlimited but periodic':

The Ziggurat of Dur-Kurigalzu, built
in the early 14th century BCE in what
is now modern Aqar-Quf, Iraq.

*If an eternal traveller should journey in any direction, he would find after untold centuries
that the same volumes are repeated in the same disorder – which, repeated, becomes order:
the Order. My solitude is cheered by that elegant hope.*[43]

Even though haunted by the spectre of the new, contemporary art is but the recurrent outcome
of man's centuries-old quest to deal imaginatively with the hodgepodge that is our world. The
museum collects and mediates the results of that pursuit that, to paraphrase the artist Marcel
Broodthaers (1924–76), will continue 'until the end of the world'.

Herzog & de Meuron's design for the expansion of Tate Modern has
a unique temporal nature. Like Robert Smithson's qualification of the new kind of monumentality
he discerned in the work of his contemporaries, and which certainly marked his own *Mirrored
Ziggurat*, the edifice looks like it is 'not built for the ages, but rather against the ages'.[44] It
resonates with both past and future, even though it is resolutely in the present. By returning
to an architectural image that stems from the cradle of civilisation, the project emphasises its
difference with the growing commodification and commercialisation of present-day culture –
and the pastiche avant-garde language of the surrounding buildings at Bankside. As candid
aficionados of traditional museums, Herzog & de Meuron have consciously rejected the often
pompous attempts to define a new typology for the museum of the twenty-first century. Yet, in

The Tower of Babel Stele
Babylon, 604–562 BCE
A reconstruction by Martin Schøyen
after an original drawing by
Andrew George.

both its material and spatial formation, their brick and concrete structure hints at the imminent prospects of a public institution in an era of determined privatisation.

The two consecutive building phases of Tate Modern point to the fact that three major truisms about museum architecture – which seemed mutually exclusive for a long time – are ever more up for critical revision. The first states that museums need to be built for the arts, the second that museums are salient programmes for architectural experimentation, and finally the third that architecture is the prime vehicle for rethinking the museum. Following their own qualification of architecture as an 'instrument of perception', Herzog & de Meuron recognise the assignment to give form and shape to the institution of the art museum as nothing less than a triple bill. In their practice, art, architecture and the museum are not made to contend with each other, but are prompted to join forces. Their projects are driven by the desire to find a mode to reconcile all three, without granting any one of them a place of prominence. The ultimate verdict, the architects acknowledged already early on in their career, lies within the experience of the public.

> The design of the building is not the architectural design invested in it by the architect or the artist. Nor is it the design, invested in it by the economist, the engineer, or the statistician. It is the design invested in it by the perceiver.[45]

Beatriz Colomina
The Museum after Art

*Art is everywhere in the street, which is the museum
of the present and the past.*
Le Corbusier, 1923[1]

In her 1990 essay 'The Cultural Logic of the Late Capitalist Museum', Rosalind Krauss identified the signature of the contemporary museum as one in which the experience of the space of the museum takes precedence over the experience of the artworks. In other words, the space between the works is more important than the experience of the works themselves. She described the experience of seeing the Panza Collection in the Musée d'art moderne de la ville de Paris, guided by then Director Suzanne Pagé, as a kind of walk in a landscape – an itinerary in which she encountered works of art (in her words, 'old friends' of the 1960s) the way one might encounter a big rock, tree or pavilion in a park, but where the overall experience of the space dominates; what is about to happen becomes more relevant than what you are seeing right now. She recalled how her guide viewed the highlight of the exhibition as its spaces rather than the individual works on display, stopping at one point in a space where you can already see the glow of another space (coming from a Dan Flavin piece). In a much earlier essay, 'Sculpture in the Expanded Field' (1978), Krauss had defined sculpture, following the structuralist logic of the double negative, as that which is 'not-architecture' and 'not-landscape'. In the face of the contemporary museum experience, it is not just sculpture that assumes this negative position but art, as exhibited, in general. And Krauss didn't seem very happy about it.

Tate Modern, which opened in 2000, a decade after Krauss's article, magnified this new logic of the museum and made millions of people happy just to spend time in a museum: make out in a museum, lie down on the floor in some kind of ecstatic contemplation, spiral down a chute, eat, drink, dance, listen to music, go to lectures, shop, meet friends and so on. The spaces between the art have become the main event. Vast circulation spaces dominate the experience with more traditional galleries in the background. And circulation is no longer between works of art. Art can be found in circulation and circulation itself can be turned into art. A quiet white room with a few static works of art becomes almost startling, as if what is on display is not just the art but also an older way of engaging with it. The line between these two worlds has been thinned down architecturally to just a doorway where tickets are checked. The world of spectacle is free, the world of contemplation has a price. And visitors are deep in the museum by the time they cross this line, if they cross it at all. It is not simply that the outside world has come all the way in, with the circulation spaces continuing the streets outside. In fact, these spaces are in some ways more active, more social and more densely populated than the streets of the city. It is a kind of utopian ideal of the street, stripped of cars, potential violence,

<< Carsten Höller
Test Site 2006
The Unilever Series commission
for the Turbine Hall.

P. Yoshiko Chuma
Performance A–Z 1982
Storefront for Art and
Architecture, New York.

cacophonous sounds, smells, street vendors, the weather, the homeless. The museum today is a hyper-controlled, theatrical space, a contemporary image of 'public space' where people perform for each other, and broadcast that performance through social media.

Curiously, both of Krauss's essays privileged minimalism to the exclusion of artists such as Gordon Matta-Clark, Dan Graham and many others who, from the mid-1970s, were experimenting more directly with the medium of architecture, trying to break away from the art gallery and the museum by engaging with buildings. It was precisely during the late 1970s and early 1980s that architecture entered the museum and gallery system. In 1978 Max Protetch, who had been exhibiting minimalist and conceptual artists, but also the work of Andy Warhol, early performances by Dan Graham, Vito Acconci and others, moved his gallery from Washington DC to New York and started to specialise in architectural drawings. In 1980 art dealer Leo Castelli put on the exhibition *Houses for Sale* for which eight international architects were invited to put their visions of the modern house up for 'sale'. Castelli felt the need to clarify that 'drawings may be purchased separately from the commission of the project'. Storefront for Art and Architecture, a non-profit gallery, opened in SoHo, New York in 1982 as a catalyst for new work and new energy. It promptly exhibited architects and artists such as Diller + Scofidio, Morphosis, James Wines, Lebbeus Woods, Steven Holl, Dan Graham, Dennis Adams, Jenny Holzer, Krysztof Wodiczko, Wolf D. Prix, Tadashi Kawamata, Mike Webb, Enric Miralles and

Carme Pinós, Mel Chin, Camilo José Vergara, Muntadas, Matthew Ritchie and Julia Scher – many of them at a very young age and all of them working at the intersection of art and architecture. The first Architecture Biennale did not take place until 1980, with the postmodern manifesto of the 'Strada Novissima' of Paolo Portoghesi in Venice (preceded by a small number of exhibitions of architecture within the Art Biennale, starting in the mid-1970s under Vittorio Gregotti). The first museums and archives of architecture are also a postmodern phenomenon and are even housed in postmodern buildings – for example, the Canadian Centre for Architecture in Montreal (1979) and the Deutsche Architektur Museum in Frankfurt (1984).

It is not by chance that at the same time that architecture started to get its own territory in museums, galleries and biennales, artists started to take over the architect's territory. In the 1976 Biennale 'Ambiente/Arte', organised by Germano Celant, Dan Graham built his *Public Space / Two Audiences*, a rectangular room with the proportions of the golden section, divided into two square chambers by a pane of acoustic glass. One of the far walls of the room was a mirror, and the wall that faced it was white. Graham likened the Venice Art Biennale and other art fairs to world fairs, in which countries have their own pavilions and art is the commodity. In Venice, he attempted to upset the system by making the audience into the exhibit. Visitors to the pavilion would see themselves seeing themselves. They become the artwork, the commodity. Graham's pavilion complicates the art scene. The viewing subject becomes the object.

Dan Graham's work is closely linked to modern architecture and to the historical figure of Mies van der Rohe through the idea of the glass pavilion. When commissioned to build the German Pavilion for the International Exhibition in Barcelona in 1929, Mies asked the Ministry of Foreign Affairs what was to be exhibited. It is a normal question for an architect: What is this building for? An artist never needs to ask that. The answer was: 'Nothing will be exhibited. The pavilion itself will be the exhibit.'[2] Interestingly, Mies was being treated as an artist. His pavilion doesn't even have plumbing. If for Gordon Matta-Clark the difference between architecture and sculpture was that one has plumbing and the other not,[3] then the Barcelona pavilion was art. It was precisely in the absence of a traditional programme that the pavilion became an exhibit about exhibiting. All it exhibited was a new way of looking. The act of viewing was itself on display, rather than objects to be seen.

Despite its prominent position in the layout of the 1929 International Exhibition in Barcelona, the Barcelona Pavilion went largely unnoticed. Even critics from professional journals passed over it entirely, unable to discern its significance. Some local journalists with no particular training in architecture provided the only testimony to its existence. They commented on the 'mysterious effect' of the pavilion, 'because a person standing in front of one of these glass walls sees himself reflected as if by a mirror, but if he moves behind them he then sees the exterior perfectly'.[4] From the inside, visitors would see people on the outside looking at themselves, in the position they had themselves just vacated. The pavilion is a place of encounter with oneself and others, an encounter with an encounter.

The Barcelona Pavilion is a kind of house, complete with front and rear entrances, a stone garden and pools, but it is a house with no interior. The inside is constructed of reflections of the outside, multiplied by the shiny surfaces of the marble, chrome and glass. The play of reflections one normally encounters in the streets of the modern city, catching one's reflected image in a shop window suspended alongside the commodities on display, is multiplied and treated as a building material. The pavilion turns the street into a domestic interior where you see both yourself and others seeing. This internalisation, even domestication, of the street could be the very project of modern architecture, and is inseparable from the project of the modern museum.

Modern architecture, it can be argued, was incubated in a series of domestic projects that were explicitly set up to exhibit modern art, and which ultimately absorbed and transformed the logic of exhibition. Indeed, the modern museum and the modern house follow the same logic. Le Corbusier's idea of the museum started with a house, the Maison La Roche, in Paris, of 1922–3.[5] The client, Raoul La Roche, a young Swiss banker and Director of the Crédit Commercial de France, was one of the major sponsors of the magazine *L'Esprit Nouveau* and commissioned its editors, painter Amédée Ozenfant and Le Corbusier, to purchase a collection of cubist paintings for him. At Le Corbusier's prodding, La Roche ended

up also buying purist paintings by both artists.[6] Once the collection was assembled, Le Corbusier talked La Roche into making a house for the paintings, writing: 'La Roche, when you have a fine collection like yours, you should also have a house built worthy of it.'[7] Modern domestic architecture was developed as a frame for cubist and purist paintings.[8]

La Roche used to open the house to the public on Tuesdays and Fridays, turning it into a private museum with public visiting hours. Soon the issue of whether what was on show was the paintings or the building became blurred, a source of conflict between Le Corbusier and both La Roche and Ozenfant. Le Corbusier wanted some of the walls to be kept free of paintings. He wrote to Ozenfant: 'The La Roche house should not take on the look of a house of a (postage-stamp) collector. I insist absolutely that certain parts of the architecture should be entirely free of paintings, so as to create a double effect of pure architecture on the one hand and pure painting on the other.'[9] La Roche responded to Le Corbusier's desire to exhibit the house itself: 'I commissioned from you a "frame for my collection". You provided me with a "poem of walls". Which of us two is most to blame?'[10] Here we already have exactly the same concern that Rosalind Krauss would voice in the face of the postmodern museum, almost seventy years earlier. The intrusion of architecture into the space for the contemplation of art is not a postmodern phenomenon but a quintessentially modern one.

The paintings in the La Roche house were hung in a specific sequence along the spiraling promenade of the house, and it is important to remember that it was precisely here, in this house, that Le Corbusier invented the *promenade architecturale* – the idea of an architecture experienced in choreographed movement along a predetermined path. The itinerary in the La Roche house was meant to guide the public past the paintings in a way that – conveniently for Le Corbusier – demonstrated the triumph of purism over cubism. This logic of exhibition through internalised promenade became most polemical in the Villa Savoye in Poissy (1928–31) where the visitor literally drives into the house and the movement continues up the spiral ramp that organises the whole experience of the house. There is no longer an art collection here, but the promenade continually opens up framed views to the inside and the outside of the house. The house is all street, neither interior nor exterior space. As Le Corbusier put it: 'In [Villa Savoye] it is a question of a real architectural promenade, offering constantly changing views, unexpected, sometimes astonishing.'[11] The inhabitants have become visitors in their own house, constantly on the move and watching others move.

Indeed, Le Corbusier went so far as to speak about the inhabitants of the modern house as 'visitors'. Writing specifically about Villa Savoye, he said: 'The visitors … turn round and round in the interior, asking themselves what is happening, understanding with difficulties the reasons for what they see and feel; they do not find anything of what is called

a "house". They feel themselves in something entirely new. And … I do not think they are bored!'[12] The occupants of Le Corbusier's house are displaced. First because they are disoriented. They do not know how to place themselves in relation to this building – it does not look like a 'house.' But also because the occupant is only a 'visitor'. Le Corbusier's subject is detached from the house with the distance of a visitor, a viewer, a photographer, a tourist … a museum-goer even. And crucially, visitors are not 'bored'. Against the nineteenth-century boredom of the interior, modern architecture is a form of entertainment.

Le Corbusier's and Mies van der Rohe's idea of the museum emerged literally out of the house.[13] Domesticity is the real source of modernity in museums. The spiraling ramps that define Le Corbusier's domestic architecture are simply exaggerated and celebrated in a kind of hyper-ramp in his museum projects. The carefully choreographed views of nature through the windows in the houses are simply replaced with the view through the frame of each painting. In each of the multiple versions of his spiral museum, Le Corbusier emphasised the surprising lateral views within the labyrinthine spaces. Viewing is what is on view.

The internalised street of the domestic projects became the museum as internalised street with Le Corbusier's 1929 project for the Mundaneum, to be built in Geneva, Switzerland. The client, Paul Otlet, a Belgian industrialist, wanted to establish an international

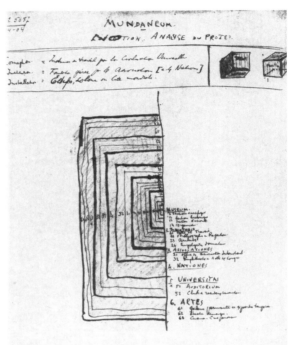

organisation of intellectuals based on a large campus which included an airport, a university, a stadium, botanical and mineral gardens, exhibition spaces, a world library and a museum: 'Our desire is that in one place on the globe the total image and significance of the world should be visible and understood; that this place should become a holy place ... a contribution from science to universal organisation.'[14] The central element of the Mundaneum was the 'world museum': a pyramid made out of a square spiral, a continuous gallery that would show the various stages of civilisation in evolution. Visitors would take an elevator to the top of the pyramid (the beginning of civilisation) and walk down the spiral ramp until they reached the ground: the present day.

Le Corbusier flattened out the spiral when he proposed a Museum of Contemporary Art in Paris in 1931. The museum is now made out of a single continuous wall folded into a square spiral. This system provided a linear exhibition space that could be extended as the collection grew. Le Corbusier's radical idea was that the museum could even be started with a collection of just one painting, with the donor also donating a length of wall. With each new painting, more wall would be added. When describing the project he insisted:

> The museum has no facade; the visitor will never see a facade; he will only see the interior of
> the museum. One enters the heart of the museum by means of an underground passage and

the wall opening for the entrance door would, once the museum has reached its full magnificent size, comprise the 9000th meter of the total developed length of the museum.[15]

The space of the traditional museum has been transformed into a length, a wall continuously folding upon itself. Only a few cuts are made in the wall to allow the visitor to break the fixed trajectory and move through the building in different ways. The museum is entered through an underground passage and the collection is to be experienced in a singular guided promenade along a seven-metre-wide space – a spiral that keeps expanding as more wall is added. Le Corbusier even recommended that 'a mason and a labourer … be permanently employed in building this museum in an interrupted and perennial operation.'[16] The endless museum would be endlessly under construction.

In 1939, Le Corbusier called his latest version of the museum for Philippeville in Algiers the 'Museum of Unlimited Growth'. The museum is an ever-expanding interior without an exterior. It is a machine for swallowing the outside. The idea that museums will continuously expand becomes the very basis of the museum and the inevitable consequence of internalising the street. Already in 1923, Le Corbusier had written in the pages of *L'Esprit Nouveau*: 'Art is everywhere in the street, which is the museum of the present and the past.'[17]

The carnivorous spiral museum became part of the civic centre of Le Corbusier's Saint-Dié town plan in 1945. In fact, Le Corbusier seemed to insert a museum of unlimited growth project wherever he went. The first version to be actually built was designed for Ahmedabad in India between 1952 and 1956. In anticipation of contemporary ideas, the Director Prithwish Neogy declared that the aim of the museum was 'to bring about the active participation of people ... instead of encouraging mere irresponsible contemplation of rare luxury objects torn from their contexts ... The objects will appear not in unique isolation but as a reality – against ... the pattern of culture that produced the artifacts.'[18] The programme included a library, open-air theatre, travelling exhibitions, audience participation, music and cinema all housed in one collection of buildings: 'The whole world was to be there', in the words of the director.[19] The museum that swallows the outside is no longer quiet. It increasingly becomes a space of performance, interaction and participation.

As the spiral project kept travelling, Le Corbusier successively added a pavilion to it for temporary exhibitions and a building for theatrical experiments that he called a 'Box of Miracles' (as in the Tokyo project for a National Museum of Western Art of 1957–9), and then a 'Spontaneous Theatre' (as in the project for an International Art Centre near Frankfurt of 1963).[20] From 1964 to1968, the project returned to India, when Le Corbusier brought yet another version of the museum to Chandigarh, and finally, in 1965, to Paris when he was commissioned by André Malraux, then Minister of Culture in France, to do a 'Museum of

Le Corbusier
Museum of Unlimited Growth, 1939
From Le Corbusier, *Oeuvre Complète*
vol.4, 1938–46.

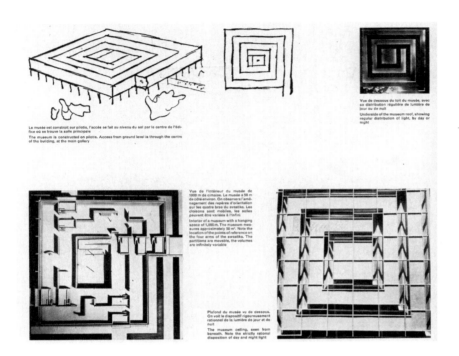

Le musée est construit sur pilotis, l'accès se fait au niveau du sol par le centre de l'édifice où se trouve la salle principale
The museum is constructed on pilotis. Access from ground level is through the centre of the building, at the main gallery

Vue de dessous du toit du musée, avec sa distribution régulière de lumière de jour ou de nuit
Underside of the museum roof, showing regular distribution of light, by day or night

Vue de l'intérieur du musée de 1000 m de cimaise. Le musée a 50 m de côté environ. On observera l'aménagement des repères d'orientation sur les quatre bras du swastika. Les cloisons sont mobiles, les salles peuvent être variées à l'infini
Interior of a museum with a hanging space of 1,000 m. The museum measures approximately 50 m². Note the location of the points of reference on the four arms of the swastika. The partitions are movable, the volumes are infinitely variable.

Plafond du musée vu de dessous. On voit le dispositif rigoureusement rationnel de la lumière de jour et de nuit
The museum ceiling, seen from beneath. Note the strictly rational disposition of day and night light

the 20th century' to be sited in Nanterre. Le Corbusier, however, kept insisting that it should be in the centre of Paris, near the Grand Palais. He dreamed of a museum of the twentieth century set on ten-metre (or higher) *pilotis* above the streets and squares of Paris. The museum would float over the world it swallowed. Le Corbusier even thought of bridging the river Seine across the Quai d'Orsay. He was at work on a version of the museum project to be placed in Nanterre when he died in August 1965 and the project was never realised. Once again, he was arguing for a square box that could grow endlessly, absorbing and classifying the entire world outside.

'The true museum is the one that contains everything', Le Corbusier wrote alongside an image of a bidet in *L'Esprit Nouveau* in 1924. With this definition, the world and the museum are conflated. Museum architecture, in the literal sense of a bounded space, an enclosure containing objects, becomes redundant. In 1951 Malraux would famously call for a 'museum without walls', an imaginary museum that comes into being with the new means of communication that allows any object to be collected without the need for a physical space. Le Corbusier's project for an endless museum tested the limits of an equally radical concept of a museum that is only wall. A museum that can be anywhere, collect anything – an architecture independent of the ground and of culture, a nomadic architecture for a globally networked world. Such a museum made of a folded street has no interior. It brings the world in, domesticating the outside rather than looking out at the world. Detached static contemplation becomes mobile social action and architecture becomes the event.

Below and opposite:
Frank Lloyd Wright
Interior perspectives
of the Guggenheim Museum
New York, 1943–57.

RECEPTION

The idea of internalising the street increasingly defined the twentieth-century museum, most obviously with the 'inverted ziggurat', as Frank Lloyd Wright described the Guggenheim Museum in New York (1943–59) to *Time Magazine* in a press conference in 1947 – even speculating that such a ziggurat could be expanded infinitely, unlike a traditional one. The spiral ramp became the gallery itself and complaints from artists, curators, critics and even the director of the museum that the architecture was intruding on the experience of art, upstaging the art, were voiced from the very beginning of the project to its completion. John Canaday, a critic for the *New York Times*, described it on the very day it opened as 'a war between architecture and painting in which both come out badly maimed'.[21] Wright kept insisting that architecture itself would be the frame for art: 'The only "framing" needed by the painting is this relationship to architectural environment.'[22] He had even called the project 'Archeseum' on all the drawings, specifications and correspondence until told to stop doing so in 1956 by Harry Guggenheim. The hostility to the building continued for a long time. Some of the many legends surrounding the building include the hip problems that its guards supposedly develop, presumably from standing on the ramp with one leg lower than the other. Ironically enough, it is only in recent years that a new generation of artists has appreciated the challenge, the push back that the building presents, happily engaging with the architecture. Interestingly enough, some of these are the same artists who feel at home in the social spaces of Tate Modern's Turbine Hall. And it is useful to remember that Wright's original vision for the

museum was also of a profoundly social space. Drawings and sketches of the project show individual paintings and other works of art being looked at by groups of people assembled in the alcoves, but most visitors are looking across the void and at each other, or down to the crowded, loungy, almost festive ground floor where most of the action is.

The Centre Pompidou of Renzo Piano and Richard Rogers in Paris (1971–7), the project that made the next quantum leap in the concept of the museum as mass medium, was – not coincidentally – another commission from André Malraux. It went one step further with the creation of a new public square in the city, which was then 'pulled' into the building to form a public library and bookshop, up the side of the building as circulation and information spaces, with the moving visitors on display passing each other on escalators in tube-shaped vitrines, and across the roof as restaurant and terraces – with the galleries sandwiched in between. The project was a watered-down version of Cedric Price's Fun Palace, the polemical project for a building without any walls that he symptomatically called 'a university of the streets'. The Pompidou brought the ever thinner line between street and gallery deeper into the museum, turning even the act of visiting the museum into a spectacle.

At Tate Modern, this entire scenario was digested and amplified, with the public square becoming a huge internal volume extended by a massive vertical circulation system including public landings with books, objects, interfaces, performances, installations, cafés, education areas, restaurants and terraces, presenting multiple occasions to congregate

Renzo Piano and Richard Rogers
Centre Pompidou
Paris, 1971–7
Axonometric drawing from the original competition plans: the so-called
'jelly-mould' scheme (ultimately
abandoned) was a development of
the original idea, in which the clarity
of the concept receded.

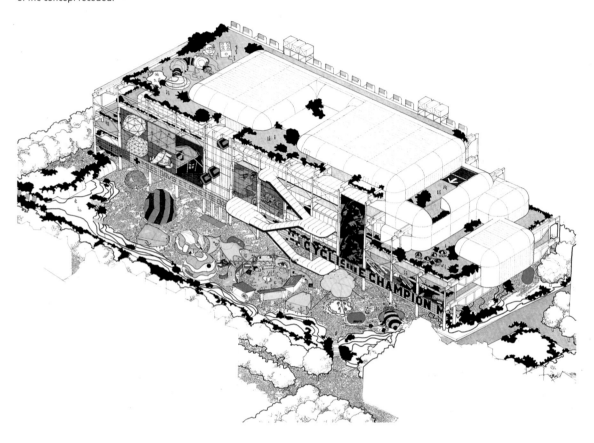

and meet other people and to look back at the city as if to situate oneself and admire it like any other work of art or installation in the collection. The most popular work in the permanent collection is the framed city of London itself – with the galleries as secondary, optional extras.

Yet something of the domestic origin of the twentieth-century museum remained. It is not by chance that Herzog & de Meuron's first project for a museum was for a private collection, a kind of house-museum in a garden in Munich to house the Goetz Collection. The very precise calibration of the galleries in Tate Modern was modelled on its spaces. The strength of Tate Modern derives from both the extreme, even monumental, embrace of public space, and the domestic refinement of the galleries. Nor was it by accident that the architects chose to photo-collage an image of Rachel Whiteread's *House* 1993 into the Turbine Hall in the competition drawings that they submitted for the museum. Whiteread turns the hidden domestic interior of a terraced house into a public sculpture, while Tate Modern is the endgame of the museum of the twentieth century that began with houses. Institutions like MoMA and the Guggenheim began with domestic rooms that were successively expanded by bringing more and more of the street inside. They have often been accused of bringing the logic of shopping arcades and department stores into the museum, for example with the escalators introduced by Cesar Pelli in 1984 in the first expansion of MoMA's original 1939 building.

The anxiety is not only about the ever more explicit treatment of art as a commodity, but also about the related possibility of bringing anything inside the museum, including an ever wider public – the world-absorbing ability of the arcades described so eloquently by Walter Benjamin. The very first page of his massive study of the arcades quotes a nineteenth-century illustrated guide of Paris on the emergence of a new internalised city, which he associates with the birth of consumerism: 'These arcades, a recent invention of industrial luxury, are glass-roofed, marble-paneled corridors extending through whole blocks of buildings, whose owners have joined together for such enterprises. Lining both sides of these corridors, which get their light from above, are the most elegant shops, so that the *passage* is a city, a world in miniature.'[23] Tate Modern inherited this interiorisation of the city project, but what is consumed now is art, or, more precisely, the experience of art, or even the experience of the space of art.

How then to expand Tate Modern? What barriers are left? What more can be absorbed before the museum explodes? With the first Tate Modern project, artists were extensively surveyed for their opinions and they all seem to have used the occasion to condemn museum architecture for interfering with art. In the meantime, the building itself has left this old view behind. With the latest project, it is notable that the artists' views were not sought. Only the public was surveyed. It is the real users of the building that matter. The visitor is treated like an artist, a performer, engaged with the museum in unexpected ways. The museum learns from the visitor as much as the visitor learns from the museum. And this new kind of interactive partner is steadily getting younger. More than half of the visitors to Tate Modern are under 35 years old. The museum that invited them in to perform is obliged to perform in return.

Once again, the ziggurat with an internal spiral movement returns to intensify the spectacle of encounter between social space and gallery, expanding the range of things that can be exhibited, the ways of exhibiting them, and the spaces of social interaction. The diversity of possible performances by artists and by visitors is increased, yet the sensitivity to the domestic remains, most evidently in the obsessive care taken with furniture, constructing a sense of home and personal space in the very heart of the public action. The addition of the brick tower, rising up from the buried tanks, grafted into the side of the existing building and reaching high above, is not just the inevitable expansion of the museum. It is an image of the very idea of the museum as an expansion device, a reaffirmation of the modern project to swallow up the outside. The endgame is not over yet – and we are not bored.

Tate Modern's ability to absorb the urban realm left all other major museums behind more than a decade ago. Having been forced to reinvent the museum of the twenty-first century because it could not emulate the collections of the classic modern museums like MoMA, Tate Modern was an experiment that turned out to be more successful than anyone could have anticipated. The expanded Tate tries to deepen the experiment, testing the limits

of internal urbanism, but it may well be the endgame of this kind of massive museum. As Tate continues to eat the streets, other museums seem to be heading in the opposite direction, getting out of their skins to occupy the streets in ever more expansive yet anti-monumental gestures that ultimately threaten big architectural statements. The proliferation of biennales, festivals, fairs, temporary pavilions and so on is bringing the museum logic to cities all over the world in a kind of urban performance. Every such pop-up event produces a kind of proto-urbanism. They create a temporary city within a city. This is obvious in old biennales like Venice with its own streets lined with pavilions, but it is equally true when installations and events are dispersed throughout a city. For each of these exhibition-events, there is a special map to guide visitors, a map through an alternative urbanism that is temporarily superimposed on the existing city. The usual urban circuits give way to new patterns and the performance of temporary architecture, like that of an artist, provokes new movements, new interactions, and new thinking. This confusion, even dissolution, of the art object into a kind of landscape experience is equally a dissolution of the line between the inside and the outside of the museum. As architecture enters the exhibition space, and systems of exhibition enter the street, new kinds of museums – or post-museums – become possible.

The River entrance to level 1 of the Boiler House.

Birch trees in the River Landscape.

The high wall on the south side of the Switch House, delineating the Tanks beneath.

The viewing terrace on level 10 of the Switch House, looking east towards the Shard.

as work progressed. Nick loves architecture and has considerable architectural talent. But in the first phase we were less receptive to such an intense exchange. We were more defensive; we were not used to laying things out on the table so freely in order to find the best possible solution together.

Chris Dercon So it was a completely new experience for you.

Pierre de Meuron As mentioned, the decision made by Nick and the jury was based on the design proposals in combination with getting to know the people behind the proposal. Nick certainly had in mind to play an active part in the coming design process, to set up fruitful and intense collaboration between client and architect. No client has ever been as personally involved in one of our projects as he was – and still is. Significantly, our strongest works often have strong and active clients.

Chris Dercon I think you were chosen because you showed, 'We do not want to change the existing building'.

Jacques Herzog We wanted to do what we try to do in most of our projects, which is to look at the givens as carefully as possible in order to identify the potentials before taking action and possibly destroying something that we might regret later. We try to reinforce what the site offers before introducing new things. You can compare this to traditional cooking. The best cook is the one that works with readily available local and seasonal ingredients and thoroughly exploits their potential before adding things from an exotic market.

Chris Dercon What did you reinforce?

Jacques Herzog I think the Turbine Hall is the most striking example. It is the key design piece on the way to creating Tate Modern. We left it empty and didn't fill it up with floors and spaces. Gilbert Scott had already set the stage for that grand open space: the turbines were presented like sculptures within it. It already looked like a museum to us. Removing the turbines allowed us to dig

The excavation
of the Turbine Hall, 1996

down to the ground and literally excavate that space – like an archaeological dig, so that you would have the entire museum right in front of you. We dug down to the level of the oil tanks, opening up this immense covered plaza for both the public and the artists. No matter where you come into the space, it says 'This is a place for art'. We absolutely wanted to convey this message.

Chris Dercon It's interesting that you say that because the success of Tate is often explained by the exact opposite: 'We are an art gallery *and* first and foremost a public space.'

Jacques Herzog Yes, that is very much part of its success. It is a public and open space for everyone, but it is also a gallery; it 'smells' of art. It is not a commercial and functional space like an airport or a shopping mall where you also find a lot of people (and sometimes even art). And unlike the latter, the people who go to Tate Modern somehow share a common interest in the broadest sense of the term; they share the desire to experience that space.

Pierre de Meuron Yes. We were fully aware of the significance of a grand and generous indoor public space, which welcomes millions of visitors. I may draw a comparison with the National Stadium in Beijing, where we had a similar line of thought. The latter was, of course, in the first instance a sports facility for a limited, very short period of time – for the Olympic Games of 2008 – but to us

it is above all a public place. The Turbine Hall and the Concourse around the
stadium are both a sort of threshold space between the outside and the inside
of the building. This defines what makes Tate Modern so attractive – and not
only to regular museum visitors.

Chris Dercon The architect and curator Terry Riley once said, when he was coaching the design-
process of the new extension of the Museum of Modern Art in New York, that one should look
for architecture which is capable of saying 'This is a museum'.

Pierre de Meuron First, we just wanted people to walk in and then, possibly,
to have an immediate encounter with art. Instead of saying 'This is a museum',
I am more interested in saying 'This is a place for art and artists and people
to come together'. Admission is free and people go there even if they are not
primarily interested in art. But it certainly does feel different from going to
a shopping mall or an airport where everything, all the smells and sounds and
sights, have the scent and intent of allure – a far cry from what Tate Modern
has to offer.

Chris Dercon I think that the first time the Turbine Hall felt really like an *agora*, where people
could decide to do whatever they wanted to do – stay for a long or short time, hang out, sleep,
have a picnic, make love – was in 2003, when Olafur Eliasson's *Weather Project* was installed.

The Turbine Hall photographed from
one of the two gantry cranes which
were preserved from Bankside Power
Station. The Level 4 Bridge is in the
distance, the Turbine Hall Bridge in
the foreground with Ai Weiwei's *Tree*
2010 installed.

A very different feel from other museums. Which do you think was the first Turbine Hall commission where you could say, 'This is what we had in mind'?

Jacques Herzog Olafur for sure, but also Anish Kapoor and certainly and very subtly Bruce Nauman – all those artists used the gallery in a way that you couldn't do anywhere else. That's what it is made for! Another reason for the success of the space is that we left its architecture raw and industrial and didn't add many signs of our own design. There is little evidence of an architect's handwriting, which can often be a bit awkward and invasive. Our main contribution was to make the space be even more like what it was already or like what it wanted to be when it was first built, namely an industrial cathedral. Even in the second phase, we didn't make much use of architectural details. It is all space and structure.

Pierre de Meuron A significant factor regarding the Turbine Hall and the building as a whole is its placement as a deliberate answer to St Paul's Cathedral on the opposite side of the Thames. The two landmarks are aligned and have a plainly visible vertical presence in the cityscape of London. So we knew from the beginning that we wanted to keep the existing chimney even though it was no longer in use, because it clearly functions as a sign. As a horizontal response to the vertical chimney, we proposed adding a new feature, the so-called 'light beam' on top of the roof, which also provides a novel view of the City of London.

Chris Dercon But to the north.

Pierre de Meuron Yes, since they face each other.

Chris Dercon A mirror so to speak. When did you start thinking about the south?

97

Jacques Herzog The bridge across the Turbine Hall connecting the northern and southern part already figured in the earliest proposals. The southern part was totally undeveloped, a rather neglected, basically dormant part of the city. It is almost inconceivable now given the unbelievable Hongkongian density and height of the surrounding towers and developments.

Chris Dercon But the south entrance couldn't be revamped because the southern part of the power station was still in use.

Jacques Herzog Yes. But the idea of opening up to the south was part of the original scheme. The scheme that we were chosen for had an opening to the south – an access that ran through the building with a plaza in the front. We just hadn't worked out the second phase in detail.

Chris Dercon When did Nick tell you they were going to do it?

Jacques Herzog Nick said from the beginning that he wanted to continue. But he also said, we may want a younger architect to think about the second phase. He couldn't promise that we would be commissioned to design the second phase as little as he could promise to be staying on. We know too well how complex these things are. I guess Nick always wanted that extension – he had the bigger picture in his mind from the very beginning, which certainly included other types of galleries and new spaces for the public. We were very keen to extend the building from the bottom up – with the amazing oil tanks as the foundation of a whole new and different art experience. We also wanted to offer visitors a more fluid means of experiencing the height, with additional views from different angles than those provided by the first phase.

I think one of the most important differences will be the way people move through the building. Nonetheless, while being different, the second phase should feel like part of one and the same building complex with its robust industrial architecture. Otherwise we would have created an imbalance between the two parts. This was a major challenge and one of the most interesting points of exchange between Nick and us, namely, how these things get connected. I don't think we would have been able to do that back in 1995.

Pierre de Meuron Speaking of movement, in the Turbine Hall, the ramp slopes down into the space and is the key point of access to the museum from the west: you do not enter the building horizontally, nor do you walk up steps. Accessing an interior space on an inclined plane generates a singular three-dimensional experience – you first walk down, you slow down, you don't have to watch your step, you decelerate, you get a first overview of the building from the inside, you get your bearings. In addition to all that, when you reach the bottom of the

ramp, you will soon have the choice of turning north to the Boiler House, or
south to the newly converted oil tanks and the new extension, the Switch House.

Chris Dercon Why did you do that?

Pierre de Meuron If you enter the building on level 0, i.e. on street level, you
have to go down one level if you want to buy tickets or go to the museum shop.
That diminishes the significance of the lower-level (-1) and prioritises the
levels above. In the present configuration, visitors can proceed continuously
through the entire building from the very bottom up to the top floor.

Jacques Herzog We see architecture like topography. And the ramp is part of
that topography. People use it casually and with ease, and children love playing
there. Large public buildings should not just offer several access points but
also 'unnecessary' places to hang out. When a building does that well, it feels
more natural.

Chris Dercon You mention feeling natural. The galleries in the older part feel rather unnatural.

Jacques Herzog The galleries in the former Boiler House section of Tate Modern
are quite classical. The modern collection calls for galleries of that kind. But, of
course, art and artists nowadays require a great diversity of spaces. At the time,

we would not have been able to design the galleries as we have now done. Not only have we acquired a lot of experience since then, but the needs of artists have also changed. Residual spaces did not come into fashion until later. We learned about such spaces through our artist friend Rémy Zaugg and his book *Die List der Unschuld* (1982), in which he describes the installation of six cubes of cold-rolled steel by Donald Judd behind the main staircase of the Kunstmuseum Basel. This location is definitely not made for art, but it turned out to be perfect for Judd's piece. Obviously, we can't design residual spaces on purpose but the topography of the new extension will offer similar angles and places.

Chris Dercon Did you speak to the late Rémy Zaugg when you were designing the galleries of Tate Modern?

Jacques Herzog We had worked with Rémy so much that a time came when we knew ourselves what we wanted to do. Rémy came to the opening. He saw a lot of his ideas fulfilled. His ideas can be seen as a powerful counterpoint to the frivolous designs of Hollein or Stirling. But he would have understood, as we have, that galleries can and should offer a great diversity. This is what the new project and its galleries will reflect.

Chris Dercon In response to these new art practices.

Jacques Herzog Exactly.

Chris Dercon They also pose very different and difficult conditions.

Both Yes.

Jacques Herzog As we said before, the architectural structure of the former Boiler House necessarily meant a linear stretch of galleries. This relatively classical arrangement also makes perfect sense for the modern collection of Tate.

Anish Kapoor's *Marsyas*
installed in the Turbine Hall:
the 2002 commission in
The Unilever Series.

But the potential of the lighting in the gallery spaces has not been maximised. I think the lighting, both artificial and natural, is problematic. When the windows are covered and the artificial light is dimmed, you get a gloomy atmosphere, which reinforces the feeling of being caught in a place – and that's a problem. I think those museums that give you a good feeling are also places where the lighting has been exploited to its full potential.

Pierre de Meuron But this can change.

Jacques Herzog Of course.

Pierre de Meuron When you design and even more so when you build a museum, you need to think in the long term. Museum directors or curators may aim at changing or altering things, for instance the natural and artificial lighting or the colours of the walls.

Chris Dercon The demand for dark rooms in museums is steadily growing. How do you go about creating darkness when museums are essentially about creating light?

Jacques Herzog New art often requires dark rooms, but we should also think of visitors' needs. People do not want to be exposed to unvarying conditions, whether they are dark or daylit. Clusters of two or three dark rooms could be interspersed on a single floor with galleries that have different lighting, generating a lively atmosphere and enhancing the pleasure of looking at art. Working on the Kramlich House and its requirements to host its major collections of video, film and other new art forms was an important learning process for us. We tried to combine art with the daily life of the client. Naturally, this wasn't possible without some compromises. Most of the dark rooms are now separated from the rest of the house, in contrast to our original proposal for undulating glass walls of varying transparency. You could look through them into the amazingly lush Californian landscape of the Napa Valley but you could also make them matte to project works by Matthew Barney, Bill Viola and many others. So you would never be in complete darkness. Very few installations by such artists require darkness for the sake of darkness. But they do need to be dark enough to allow the image to be seen.

Chris Dercon Those are very different conditions.

Jacques Herzog Yes. And I think, technically speaking, we will be able to do that someday. Viewing an art installation in a dark space is a very different thing from watching a film in a cinema. In the museum, you see other people looking, you can stay or go and you don't have to sit down from beginning to end.

Chris Dercon Tate Modern with its Turbine Hall has given rise to a new type of work, which both architectural critics and art theoreticians often describe as 'big' but also as 'spectacle'.

Jacques Herzog I think our role as architects is to discover and offer potential. The Turbine Hall is a case in point. Its size is adequate for its role as a public agora and as a gallery for extraordinary installations. Does it invite or seduce artists to do exceptionally spectacular things? Who knows? But, as I said, we were certainly impressed by the way such artists as Olafur Eliasson or Anish Kapoor made use of the venue. Kapoor literally even stretched the space.

Chris Dercon Bruce Nauman?

Jacques Herzog Yes, his was perhaps the most radical and poetic contribution. Nauman made a very still, tranquil installation which used the dimensions of the space without relying on overwhelming scale. It was anti-spectacle. Big and spectacular installations are not necessarily a function of the dimensions of the Turbine Hall. I used the word 'potential' to express opportunities that an architect can ideally identify in a public project, which transcend the functional specifications of a brief. I think 'potential' is the right word in this context as well especially since it also implies the challenge of recognising and implementing that potential in a natural, unforced way. Today our lives are increasingly dominated by ideologically and functionally controlled spaces. Public space which is more receptive to unexpected and innovative performances is suspect and rare. That is where art can play an important role in the future, transcending its commercial role as merchandise with gigantic price tags. Art should be the opposite. Art and architecture should be about offering 'potential'. A good example is the Serpentine Pavilion Programme. It is open-ended, like Tate Modern. It is an intriguing approach and we like the idea of offering architects the opportunity to reinterpret the same park every year, so that visitors can enjoy it in a new and different light.

Chris Dercon The enormous success of Tate Modern has also had a side effect. There is rampant development all around the museum, a lot of high-rises housing expensive living quarters and businesses. And yet many flats there as well as elsewhere in London are empty.

Pierre de Meuron Purchased purely as an investment.

Jacques Herzog We should have invested there ourselves …

Chris Dercon Right, we should have bought more.

Jacques Herzog That was a strategic mistake …

Chris Dercon What else could have been done in terms of architecture?

Pierre de Meuron We had to develop a compelling building, capable of bearing up against any unpredictable future urban development. In London, you can hardly control or influence what is happening around you, and in the case of Tate Modern the ongoing fast development beat the clock. In this respect, it was undoubtedly the right decision to hang on to the chimney of the former power station and also as much as possible of Gilbert Scott's original building. Often renovations or conversions are undertaken without the requisite care, to such an extent that one can barely recognise what the building once looked like. To use the same cladding for the old building and the new extension, namely bricks, was the right decision too. It has unified the entire complex so that it can stand up to its neighbours. If, as in a previous phase of the project, we had worked

in glass and steel, the new extension would have become an undesirable ally of
the development around it. In not doing so, Tate Modern 2 has become an erratic
mineral block in the midst of the surrounding commercial environment.

Chris Dercon It connects Tate Modern with the 'weaker' neighbours, such as the dormitory
of the LSE and the council housing.

Pierre de Meuron This is well observed; the existing brick buildings back each
other – the brick as the backbone. But equally important in terms of maintaining
one's ground is the fact that the extension building is a museum from bottom
to top, from converted oil tanks to the topmost floor. Tate Modern does not use
its height to generate money, does not sell the upper floors as apartments with
empty beds. This would put a damper on a vibrant cultural institution.

Chris Dercon Harry Gugger, who worked on the first Tate Modern with you, said in an interview
in *UrbanRESET* in 2012 that it would not be possible, given today's economic and political
circumstances, to make the same building because it's too simple.

Jacques Herzog Or too archaic?

Chris Dercon Too weird, too strange?

Jacques Herzog It's archaic, which is what Pierre tried to explain with the brick. But the interior structure is rough and archaic as well. It grows out of the specific world of the oil tanks, which is indeed a rough, industrial world. This simplicity and archaism are real assets, especially as a contrast to the increasingly commercial world expanding outside in the immediate neighbourhood of the building. Once it opens Tate Modern will be even more attractive; people will experience it as a world of otherness. It will certainly be different from the way art and architecture are ordinarily experienced in comparable institutions.

Chris Dercon The architectural theoretician Mark Wigley once suggested that we need to accept the strangeness of art in the architecture for art as well. But how far can you go? The strange products some of your colleagues build do not always come out well. You, Jacques, criticised Frank Gehry once.

Jacques Herzog Every project, I think, has to respond to a specific time and place. Gehry's Guggenheim in Bilbao has transformed the city and made it a popular tourist attraction. That's a huge achievement and will turn the museum into a monument that will survive our time. But the building has also been criticised for its oversized galleries and its overwhelming architectural impact on the art. I understand that criticism, and that architectural approach would certainly have been inappropriate in the case of Tate Modern. It would have been ridiculous to make invasive inroads into such a powerful existing structure as Gilbert Scott's power station. The building, as we found it, had its 'strangeness', as you call it, and this very strangeness is what makes it such a powerful personality, capable of standing up to the commercial world around it. It seems the right building for that place. Architecture is site-specific.

Pierre de Meuron And time-specific.

Jacques Herzog Yes, time-specific, too: it needs to be right today and if it is, it is also likely to work in the future. As soon as you say, 'Oh, we must think of future trends, anticipating how we will use the building in fifty years', then you are lost. The only thing you can do is to make it work right now, for the needs of artists and people today.

Pierre de Meuron Making it work now does not necessarily mean pitting the old against the new. On the contrary, we wanted to bring the two parts as close together as possible without mimicking the old because, otherwise, a 'divorce' between the two might have been the consequence, with the extension having an affair with its newly-built neighbours.

Jacques Herzog There are two things that we abandoned in the course of the design process: the typology of stacked cubes and glass as the main material.

Sketch of the 'stacked cubes' design
for the Switch House, c.2006: an
earlier version with the stacked glass-
clad boxes, before the architects
decided to go back to an extruded
pyramid form.

We felt less and less comfortable with the design and it was a relief to realise
that we had come up with a much better, more natural solution.

Chris Dercon What does it mean when architects say 'We felt less and less comfortable'?

Jacques Herzog Design is a process that takes time. We were lucky enough to
have that time in the second phase and we used it intensely, together with Nick
Serota, to identify all those ingredients and aspects that we've been talking
about. Everything seems so obvious now, but it was been a prolonged process
with a lot of detours. For instance, the shape or the material of the building –
for quite a while, we believed a pile of stacked galleries in combination with
other spaces was the right building typology.

We had been working on 'stacks' for another project in our office. We liked
them; stacking boxes of different sizes and portions seemed a good way to
accommodate the complex brief for Tate Modern 2. We felt we could really
create an unexpected new form. It expressed total freedom – that's what we
thought. But that impression proved to be wrong. What seemed to allow
such freedom of movement inside turned out to be rather rigid and inflexible.
What we needed was a fluid and free promenade for visitors throughout the
new building as a complement to the more linear setup in the first building.

Sketch of the Switch House design,
c.2008: the later version with
horizontal layers of brick.

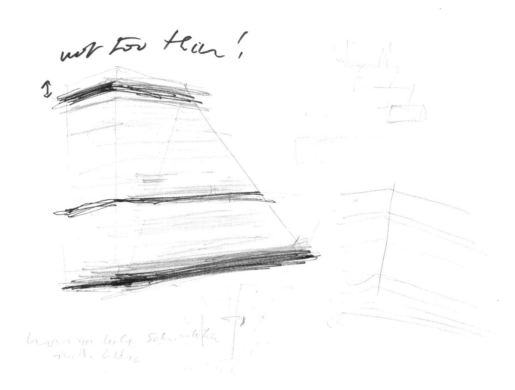

We therefore 'dissolved' the stacked sugar cubes and adopted the pyramidal
tent structure that we have now.

Pierre de Meuron Yes, what is it that makes you feel uncomfortable? From
when on do you feel more comfortable? Generally speaking, when we develop
a project which is not yet physical, built reality, we have to anticipate as
much as possible, we have to envisage untold possibilities or outcomes by
exchanging ideas, making sketches, building models and creating digital images
to visualise a not-yet-built reality as precisely as we possibly can. Between the
two of us – Jacques and I – and with and within our teams, we constantly invite
questions and objections as a means of clarifying the issues. In the case
of Tate Modern 2, we wanted to find a new form – a prism. We took the various
parameters into account, breaking them down and studying them meticulously
until the final form practically found itself. Inside, we wanted to offer visitors
free flowing circulation through the new building and that was incompatible with
our original idea of stacking boxes. The tent-like form that we finally decided
on offers much more freedom in arranging the spaces inside.

Chris Dercon People think the shape of the building is strange. Some call it a pyramid,
or even the Tower of Babel, a piece of rock or a quartz, some see a pentagram, but nobody
has mentioned a tent.

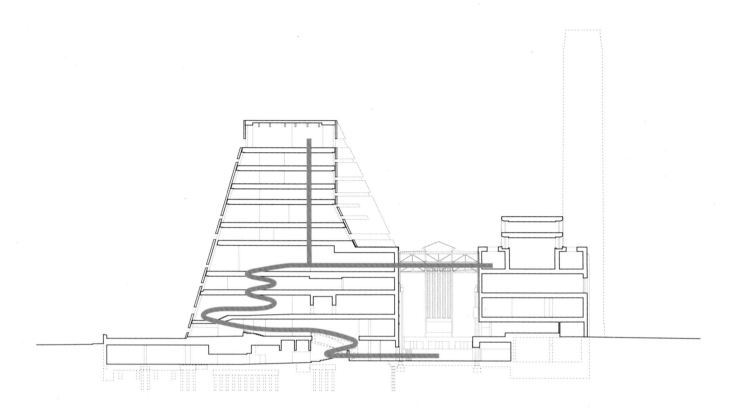

Pierre de Meuron I'm using the word 'tent' for the first time in this connection.

Chris Dercon Just checking!

Pierre de Meuron I think we all three like the idea that people see the building in very different ways and give it different interpretations.

Jacques Herzog 'Tent' may not sound quite right for such a substantial building, but it's certainly right for the inside and the freedom of movement there.

Pierre de Meuron And again, talking about a tent, in the new building there is less of what you might call the 'classical gallery' and more of a 'museum experience'. For instance, in contrast to the first phase, there is greater emphasis on spaces for educational and social activities.

Chris Dercon But there were also more practical reasons for not making a zigzag tower with so many corners, such as limitations due to 'right of view'. Was that a problem?

Pierre de Meuron No. We are used to facing problems and constraints and we can handle them. Sometimes they even generate unexpected, innovative solutions.

Chris Dercon Which were the biggest constraints? Was money a constraint?

Both Yes and no!

Chris Dercon Was money a constraint for the first Tate Modern?

Vector diagram through the Switch
House. The way through the building
orientates the visitor on each floor.

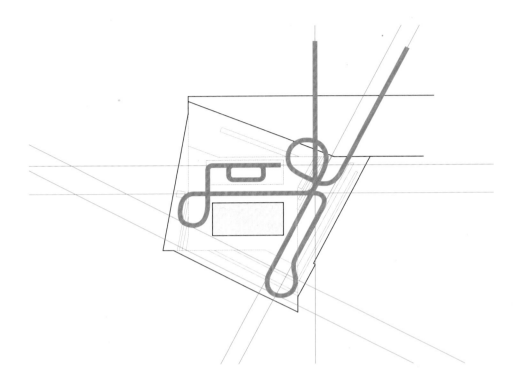

Pierre de Meuron Somewhat, but not substantially. For example, we would
have liked to install a skylight above the Turbine Hall. This feature has become
very relevant because, looking down from the new building onto the old, all
you see is the cheap roof.

Jacques Herzog But that was the only constraint, I would say.

Chris Dercon You worked with Günther Vogt on the landscape of both the north and the
south. Jasper Morrison designed the furniture and Ian Cartlidge was responsible for the
circulation and signage.

Pierre de Meuron We worked with Günther more than with Jasper or Ian. In
fact, we often work with him. It's a fruitful, mutual learning relationship and
we enjoy listening to one another. He has a real interest in plants and is very
knowledgeable about them, which Jacques and I are not. This knowledge is
crucial to his designs – more so than form.

Chris Dercon While there is less and less money for the public sector, private citizens
are building their own private museums.

Jacques Herzog That's true. Of course there is much more money than ever
before in the private sector. But history unfortunately shows that private
museums tend to run out of money and then become a burden for the state.

Pierre de Meuron And there is another factor: museum attendance is steadily growing, leading to a situation which is very different from that of twenty to fifty years ago. This also affects museum architecture. In addition, budgets for cultural activities are in decline all over the world. Some museums are running on empty. Take TEA in Santa Cruz, Tenerife, which we built in 2006: the gallery spaces are highly underused. This museum, like many others, was too big to begin with, a typical phenomenon in Spain even before the economic crisis hit the country.

Chris Dercon So we have to make museums smaller?

Jacques Herzog Shrinking the size and scope of a museum might be an option. The TEA in Tenerife could be a case study for that problem.

Pierre de Meuron Smaller, yes, but also more flexible to change and modification.

Chris Dercon What's the future of Tate Modern? Our audiences are already using the museum in many different ways. That will also be reflected sooner or later in the organisation.

Jacques Herzog Museums are, as we said before, places where art and people come together – that is and will remain their principal role. I don't think you want to adapt their programme just for the sake of attracting more and more visitors with entertainment that is not art-related. However, I do believe that especially big institutions like Tate Modern have to adopt a kind of topography of art and architecture rather than being traditional museum buildings as in the past. The expanded Tate Modern will certainly be such a heterotopic topographic place

with a real variety of programmed and unprogrammed spaces for visitors
with different needs.

Pierre de Meuron The Turbine Hall was a non-programmatic part of the first
building, which really did exploit its potential as a place to have new art
experiences. The same will happen along the *parcours* we laid out in the new
Tate Modern. Visitors will find a lot of unexpected places and unexpected art
experiences. That is what we are striving for.

Chris Dercon Isn't it an amazing privilege to be able to work on the same museum for such
a long time? I cannot think of any other architects who actually built and then extended the
same museum. It's a work in progress, really. Would you like to continue working on Tate Modern?

Pierre de Meuron A museum – a building in general – is never finished.
Right now it would be unrealistic to think about another extension. But we
might be asked to undertake smaller interventions since we understand
how the building is used. Like water that carves its way through a landscape.

Chris Dercon Like the tides of the River Thames. Going back and forth.

Pierre de Meuron Yes.

Chris Dercon Museums have to invest in digital programming and learning, they have to invest
in social media. Should architects also explore the digital expansion of museums?

Jacques Herzog I see these things rather as invisible or ephemeral traces
in the given physical context of the museum. I don't necessarily see this as
something that requires a new museum typology.

Pierre de Meuron The physical art experience will never fade away. Digital
media can complement but never replace it.

Chris Dercon Günther Vogt said in our interview, 'Tate Modern is probably the last museum
of its generation.'

Jacques Herzog I don't know, does he mean its archaic gravity or that kind
of strong personality? I am sure that artists love to show their work at Tate
Modern because of its gravity and otherness. It is a challenge but also a great
opportunity for every artist. Tate feels rooted and so does the art, once you
install it in the right place. Good work looks good in it.

End.

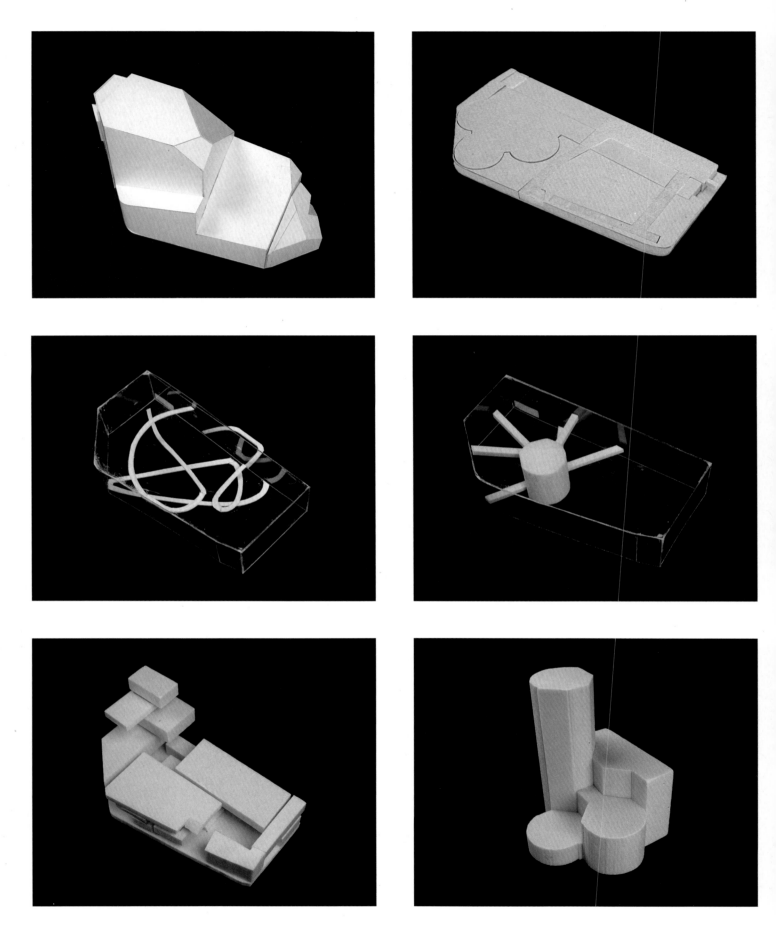

114   A selection of the architects' model studies for the Switch House, 2004–13, in chronological order: left to right, top to bottom, by page.

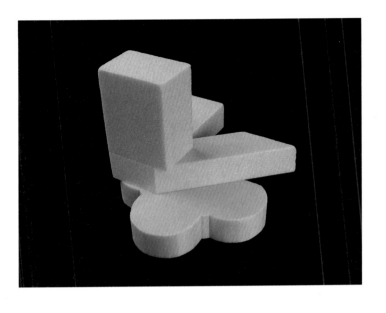

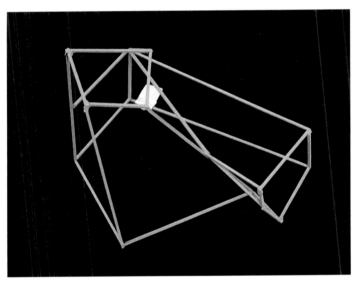

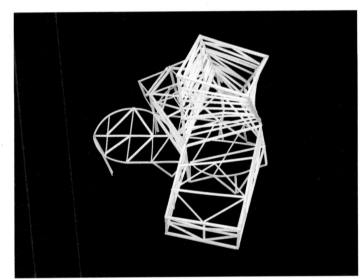

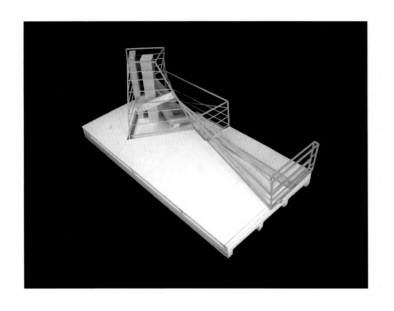
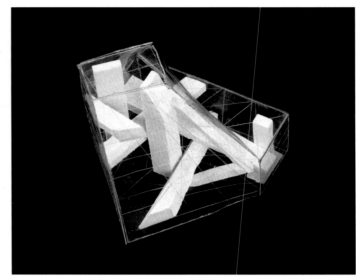
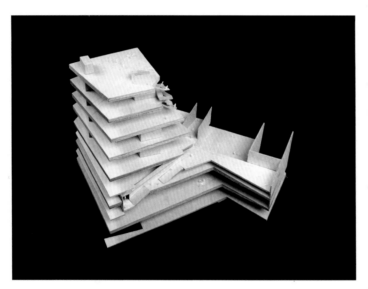
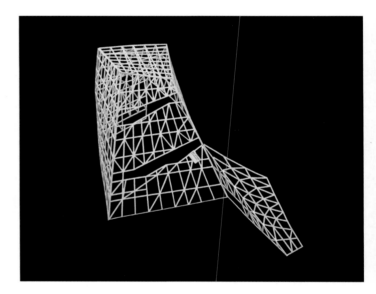
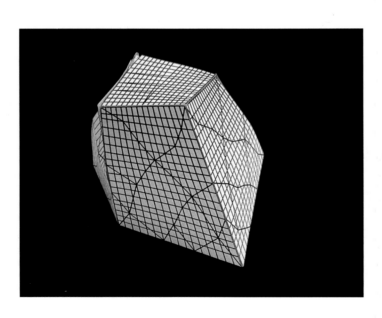
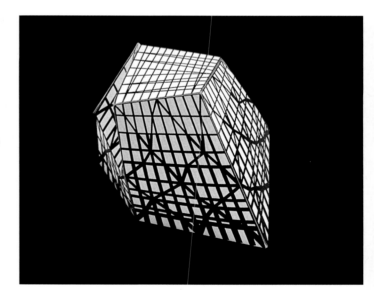

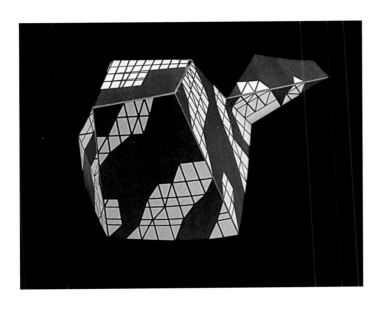
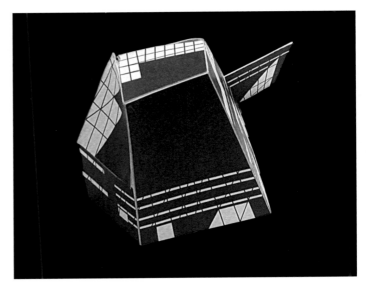
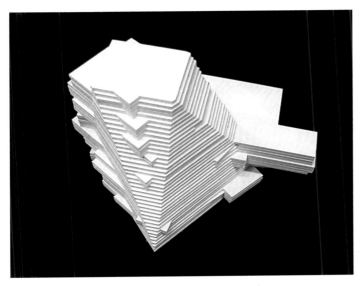

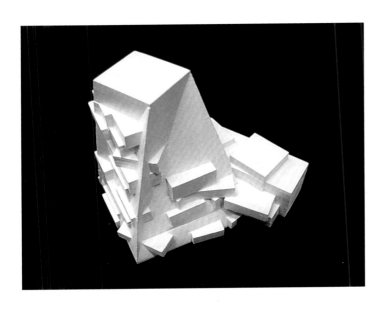
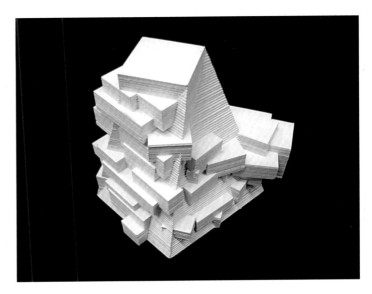

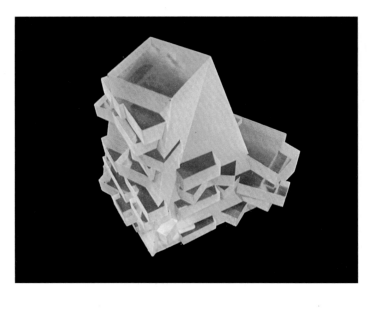
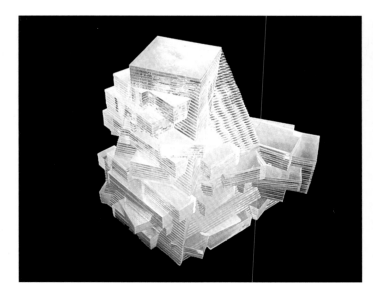
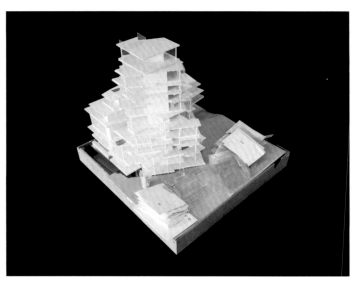
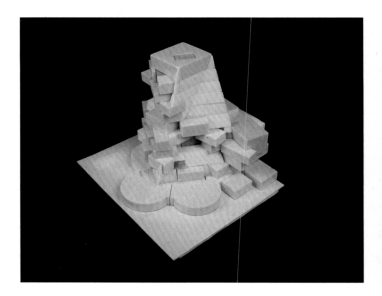

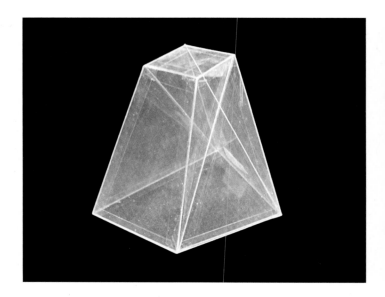

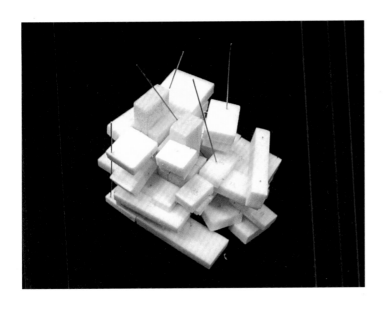

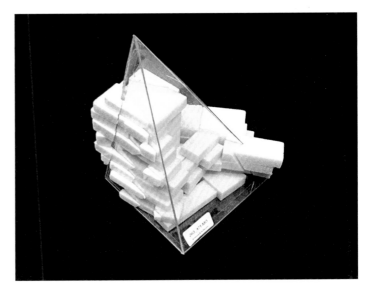

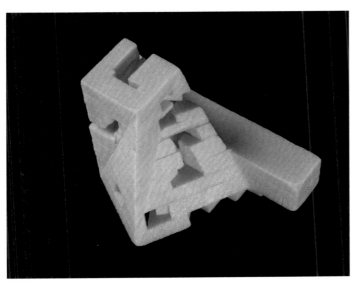

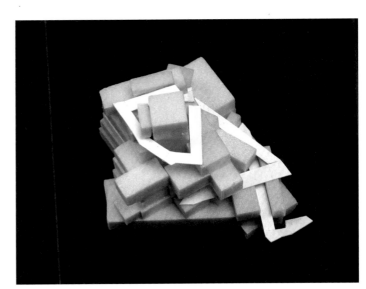

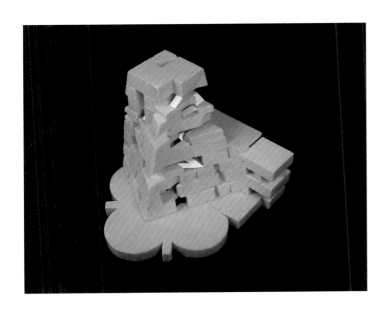

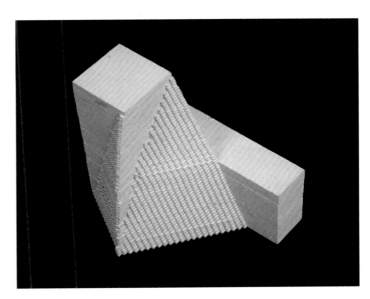

119

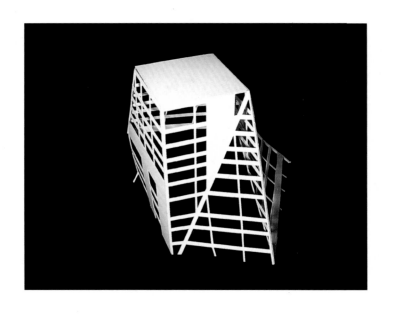

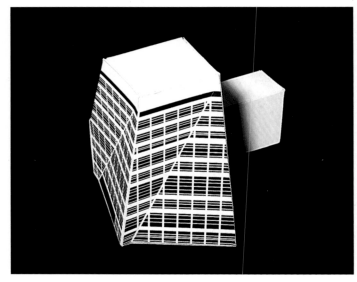

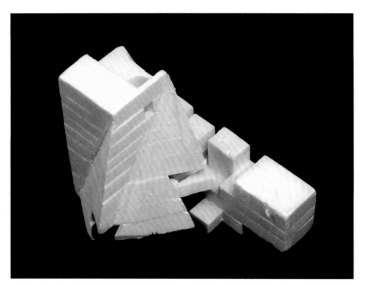

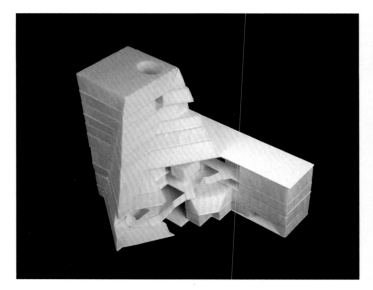

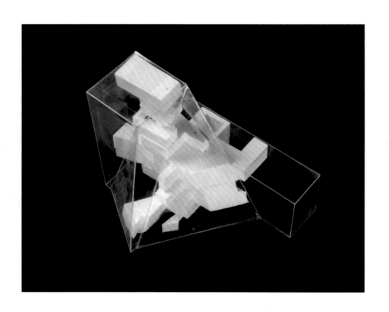

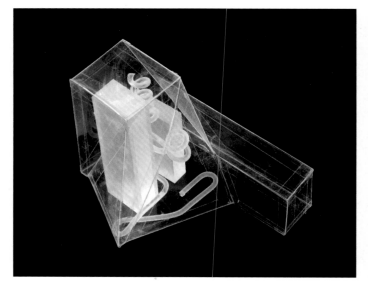

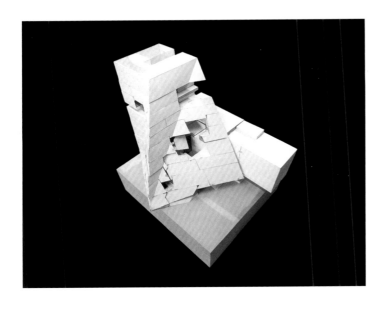
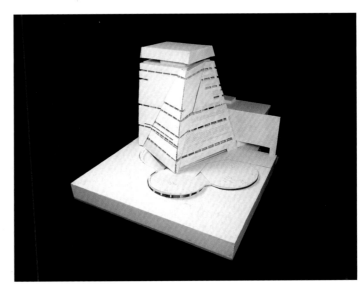

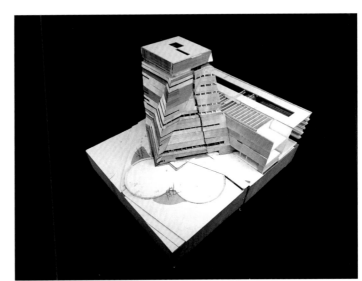
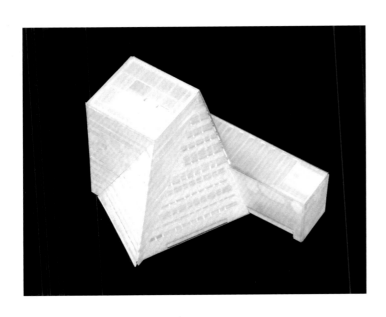

Initial concept sketch of the
landscaping for the new Tate
Modern, 2008.

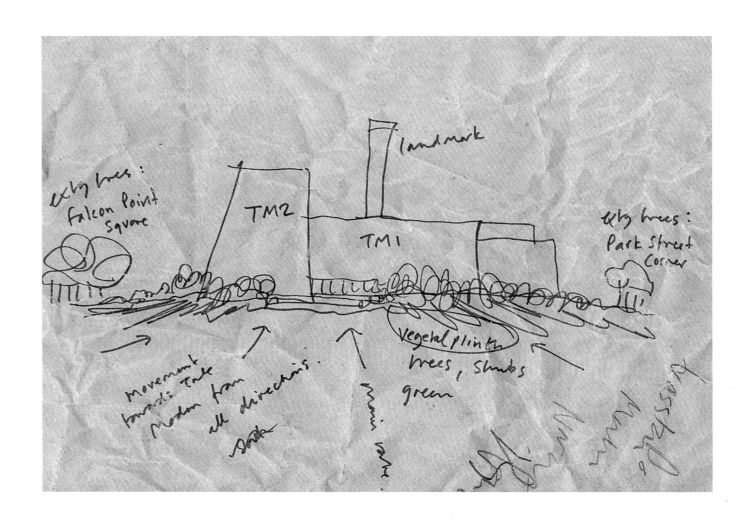

Günther Vogt
in conversation with
Chris Dercon

Chris Dercon The landscape of Tate Modern responds to the concept of landscaping in Great Britain, which is first and foremost about creating nature.

Günther Vogt It's completely different in continental Europe: in Germany, the concept of *Landschaft* is a political expression whilst in France, *paysage* is more related to agriculture. It's about creating political, social and economic identities. When we started to work for Tate, it took us about two or three years to understand that they weren't keen on this kind of structured organisation of nature. In the English tradition, landscaping has to relate to nature; think of a field of grass, a group of trees or a small forest. There are also many other intrinsic differences with the European tradition of landscaping. In England, for instance, there is the traditional 'right of way', which came about after the Industrial Revolution, when workers fought to get accessibility to the land. This wasn't the case in Switzerland, Germany or France, where you cannot cross every field because it's private land. Because of this 'right of way', in England common ground was traditionally seen as belonging to everybody. Today, however, nature no longer belongs to everyone. In contemporary London there's barely any public space left. And when you design or build something in public, after three or four years things get damaged. Nobody really feels responsible for looking after public spaces. In Switzerland, Germany or France landscape and public spaces are more protected. People really feel, 'It's our money that has been spent; it's our common ground.' Besides in London you never really know what's public and what's private. Which is the newest public space in London, for instance?

Chris Dercon The Olympic Park?

Günther Vogt Yes, but it was public only for a few weeks. The Olympic Park is mainly about private investment. Now the terrain is becoming privatised – some of it feels almost like a gated community.

Chris Dercon How did the notions of publicness and the water of the river influence the landscaping or the nature of the north and the south sides of the new Tate Modern?

Günther Vogt People living in London – let's say young people – like to go to the outside of Tate Modern. Once there, they will ask themselves, 'Could what's going on inside be interesting for me?' Then they go into the museum. Tate Modern is a place in the city to go to and to be. That was our idea also, and it

∨ Sketch made in 2008 by Vogt Landscape of the extent of London's Quaternary fluvial deposits and London Clay.

> Bankside Urban Forest, 2007. This development framework for Bankside's public realm, produced by Witherford Watson Mann Architects in 2007, focuses on local characteristics and improves pedestrian ebb and flow, towards and away from the Thames.

Vogt's scheme enables people to move intuitively through the site, along new footpaths connecting to existing routes that extend into Southwark and beyond.

really works. In fact it works too well: there are too many people on the lawn and everywhere else. What people really like is the Turbine Hall. The public sees this as a true public space, as an *agora*. Originally we wanted to create much more seating: people like to sit down in public spaces, both inside and outside.

Early on, I couldn't believe that London wasn't designed with the river in mind, looking onto the river. Unlike the Seine in Paris or the Tiber in Rome, the Thames was always in the background. In the last ten or fifteen years this has changed completely. Now there are new buildings orientated towards the river as a landscape feature. The tidal residue, even if it's very muddy, is a beautiful form of nature. The tides are there every day. Whenever I came here, I thought, 'Why are people not interested in this?' But British people don't see it, because it's so normal to them. So this was an important relationship to work with. We created

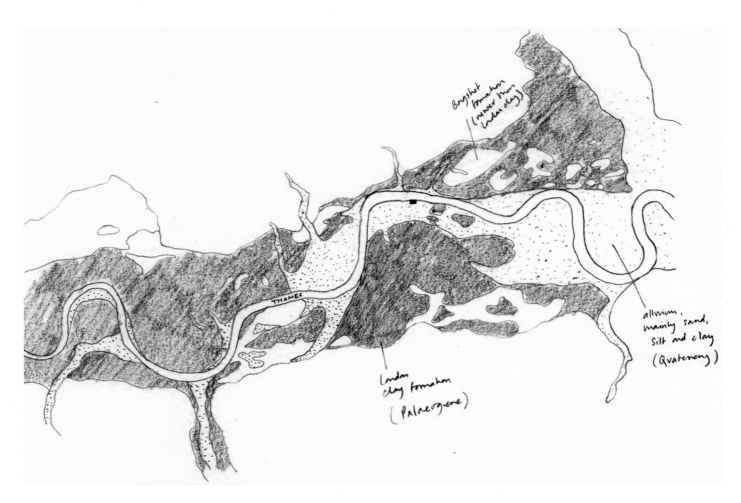

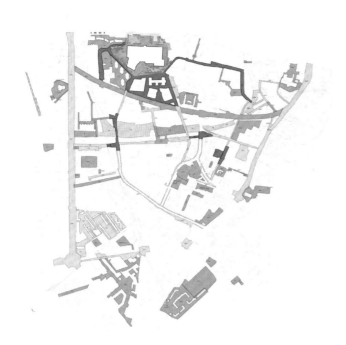

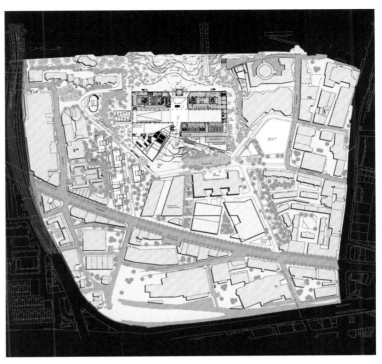

a view of the Thames that was hitherto invisible. The landscaping of Tate Modern works with nature, and is about nature; with the river and about the river, its tides, its colours and its sedimentation. Then the bridge came, connecting the north and south banks of the river. All of this is a spectacular combination. So over time you witness the making of a place, a very open place which can be activated by its users.

It's like the deliberate emptiness of the Tempelhofer Feld in Berlin, an enormous grassy field where the landing strip of the airport used to be, where many different things can happen at the same time. You can animate the field; it can be super quiet and then the next day – boom! – it's vibrating and full of life. I'm often asked, 'But what did you *do* at Tate Modern?' Almost nothing, yet it works perfectly, it comes alive. This is why I loved Rem Koolhaas's idea for the Parc de la Villette in Paris (1982–3), of not doing anything. Let it be, let it be used. Rem's idea really was to read the landscape as a programme, to be activated by the users. This was completely new in the 1980s and it still is today.

Chris Dercon Another influence for you was the conceptual art of Dan Graham. Why are his pavilions so important for you?

Günther Vogt Because he makes so many connections. He is constantly re-imagining suburban gardens and horizontal suburbia and mirroring this in many different directions. There's always a new reading, like a microscope that explores nature. You need help to see nature in detail. Graham's pavilions connect landscape and built space, from the Baroque to today.

Chris Dercon At Tate Modern, there's the water of the river, there's the lawn, there are minerals and birches. Is that nature? Is that enough?

Günther Vogt We would have liked to have done more, but there's always the question of budget. I would like to make even more of the natural space, linking

< *Hedge Two-Way Mirror Walkabout*, 2014, Dan Graham and Vogt Landscape, Metropolitan Museum of Art, New York. In this rooftop installation the suburban garden is in the foreground, Central Park in the middle distance, the New York skyline in the far distance, and – in ones mind's eye – the suburban gardens of New Jersey beyond.

∨ The Tempelhofer Feld in Berlin is so large that it is in effect a landscape within a city. Berliners voted in a referendum, won by a large majority, to leave the former landing strips of Tempelhof Airport empty, to be used as a recreation ground – no landscaping, no buildings, no programmed activities other than those of its users.

things organically with the embankment and the tides of the river, corresponding with the fluctuations of the Thames and the original site to the south before industrialisation. It was, in any case, important to have the birch trees. Many people ask why we went for these particular trees. It's mainly because of the former industrial nature of the site along the river. The poor, salty soil makes birches an obvious choice. They're strong trees. And because of the river we planted them in groves instead of lines or a grid. It's super-natural and super-artificial at the same time. It's an image. There are wonderful paintings of birch trees, not least because they're black and white.

Chris Dercon And there's the flickering of the light: birches literally visualise the wind.

Günther Vogt There's also a little bit of sound if the wind is very strong. But it's not a loud sound – it is such a discreet tree, but it still has an impact.

Chris Dercon The new walls on the south side make quite an impact. They literally enclose a vast plaza, a hard surface, much in contrast to the lawn on the north side. Why are the walls so high?

Günther Vogt The contours and the critical mass of the oil tanks were to be made visible. The tanks were originally sticking out 1.5 m above ground, so the height of the walls correspond to this. We also wanted to give it a robust form, a form of otherness. The morphological character and the height of the Tank walls express a critical difference between the human body and the scale of the building. They are construing a local horizon and not a metropolitan horizon. The colours are based on earth and clay, as are the bricks, yet the difference is a natural versus an industrial production.

Section of the terraced landscape that was originally proposed in 2008/9. It is very rare to have such a natural feature breaking into the centre of a city, so the idea was to incorporate the river's tides. The first terrace would be accessible only at low tide, whereas the other terraces would remain accessible at all times.

Chris Dercon Are you happy with the way people use the landscape around Tate Modern?

Günther Vogt At first I couldn't believe that here it's not like in continental Europe; think, for instance, of the front of the Centre Pompidou in Paris, where you have a crowded plaza. It was not our idea to suggest a lawn; Tate said, 'We need a lawn.' British people have a strong, direct relationship with grass.

Chris Dercon You once called it an 'erotic relationship'.

Günther Vogt Yes, they love to touch the grass. I saw people who after twenty minutes of rain were sitting on the lawn again – you would never see such a thing in continental Europe! This direct contact with nature is important. You feel like you are *in* the landscape. Additionally there's the idea of commons. In continental Europe, you have these commons always on the edge of cities: former military training grounds, former industrial fields and so on. You need just a lawn and some trees and something interesting will happen. That was our original idea many years ago for the landscaping of the Tempelhofer Feld in Berlin. And when I proposed this sort of 'emptiness' to the city's administration, they were ready to kill me. I said, 'This field is an urban landscape, not a park.' Recently the same idea was voted for by the people of Berlin: a great majority wanted to keep the field like it was. Now it has become one of the most popular spots of Berlin.

Chris Dercon There is a lot of talk in London about the idea to make a garden bridge over the River Thames. It seems to be a popular idea.

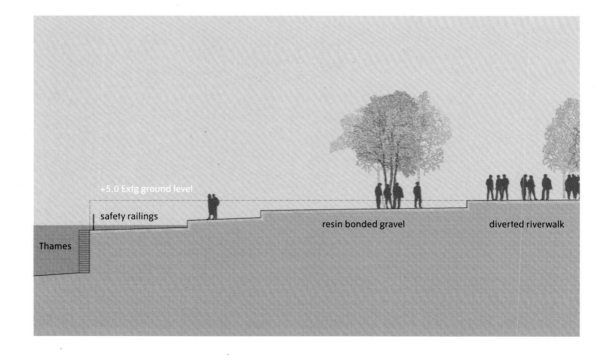

The northern landscape lawn. The idea of common ground has a long history in Britain, allowing public access to certain areas of land. This principle is reactivated and strengthened to make this public space at Tate Modern.

Günther Vogt A city like London seems constantly to need new features and fixtures – not least because of received ideas about tourism and event culture – like the O2 arena, the London Eye, or Anish Kapoor's enormous tower at the Olympic Park, which has now been turned into a slide by Carsten Höller. In terms of new bridges, there are already so many over the Thames that you sometimes don't see the river.

Chris Dercon Have you never proposed anything *in* the Thames?

Günther Vogt There was this former oil platform that Tate could have had for £1. But it was too expensive to demolish it and build something new. We wondered about turning it into an island, a garden in a container. At low tide, you could have entered the garden by passing through the mud. Tate Modern is strong enough by and for itself, though, and it doesn't need a special statement feature, such as an enormous Richard Serra sculpture out the front. What I did like about the island idea was the early twentieth-century feel of it, like the Ferris wheel and other attractions on Coney Island in New York.

Model of the southern landscape.
The features in pale blue were to be
long benches.

Chris Dercon What would be an ideal waterfront for you?

Günther Vogt When we started to work for the Tate, the waterfront was totally blocked. The relationship with the Thames was not a given, but people understood that it was necessary to make the river accessible. It's not a question of design. It's to do with reality, bending reality a bit, hacking at reality, as it were. I'm interested in public promenades. The walks in London are very interesting. It's not a classically beautiful city, but it is very interesting. The new waterfront makes it possible to discover London in a new way. Again it's much more about programming than about design.

Chris Dercon Do you like banners?

Günther Vogt Yes. I live in Switzerland. All our cantons have banners. We like flags. With a flag you control the air. It's like being in front of an army: as long as the flag is up, you're still alive. Banners are the modern translation of a very old-fashioned idea.

Chris Dercon You have a love-hate relationship with street furniture, with garden and park furniture.

Günther Vogt Oh yes. Many cities now have specially designed skater parks, but skating was originally an anarchic revolution against the architecture of the 1960s. For instance, in Switzerland skaters were outside the big shopping markets at weekends, where there's a lot of concrete and tarmac and no cars. So they could really do their own thing. And nowadays it's all stainless steel, overly designed in new parks. What is the right furniture? My response is: something

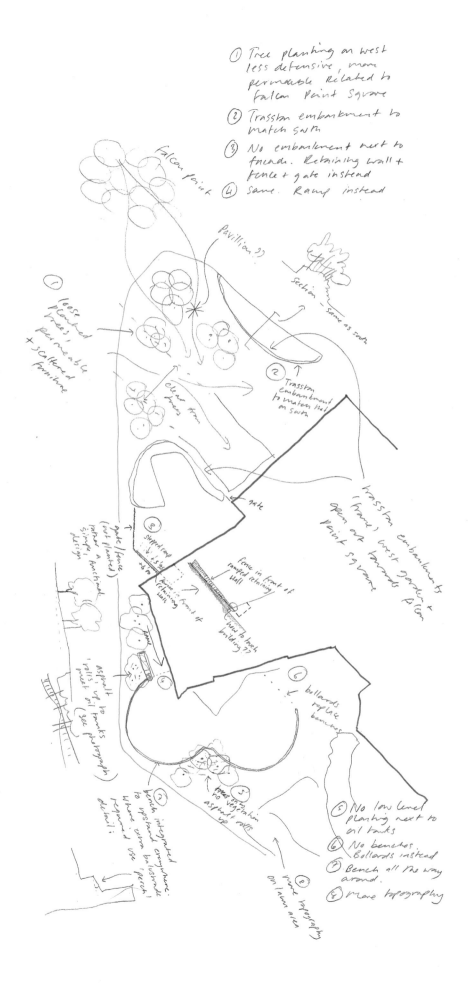

Initial concept sketch by Vogt Landscape for the second phase of landscaping, 2008.

that's not seen as furniture. Take a bench: you just sit there by yourself but twenty other people can also sit there. I like extended benches. We're constantly working on this. Yet, in general, people still have an old-fashioned, bourgeois idea about how to sit outside. It isn't accepted to show that you have free time.

Chris Dercon You like to create views. The view on to the roof of the Turbine Hall is still a blank.

Günther Vogt Yes, we originally planned to 'landscape' the rooftop too. In the whole of the Anglo-Saxon world, rooftops seem not to be important; they're just technical infrastructure. That's a shame. In Zürich, all roofs are now completely green. It's a matter of ecology and respecting nature. It has even become a legal requirement. They're a bit of a fashion now, these urban gardens, so my question would be, 'Can we also turn them into a social idea?' Green rooftops are very different from green walls. I like to compare these with the Arts and Crafts Movement. In the end, green walls are just ornament, and this doesn't move us forwards.

Chris Dercon One of the biggest problems for our cities, parks and waterfronts today is tourism on a massive scale. What can you do as a landscape architect to help to solve the burdens of tourism?

Günther Vogt Tourism is challenging London in many different ways. Yet the real treasure in London is the Green Belt. I could imagine activating parts of the Green Belt in new ways. But this is very much a public transport problem. There's huge potential there. And again, it's a question of hacking into reality – to change the realities of the organisation of our cities a bit. So landscape architecture is not a standalone. It's an interdisciplinary practice, where many realities come together.

Chris Dercon Just like with Tate Modern. Tate is like an urban culture factory.

Günther Vogt I think it's the last museum of its kind, of its generation. There will be no other chances to do this, as the notion of public funding, public domain and of publicness *per se* is going down the drain.

< Pebbles on the Thames beach.

∨ Artefacts found on the Thames shoreline, including horse bones, antique medicine bottles, pottery shards, Roman coins and flint arrow-heads, some of which were used by artist Mark Dion for his installation *Tate Thames Dig*, Tate Modern, 1999.

> The colours of the ground and of the southern wall are partially based on the river sedimentation. The roofs of the subterranean Tanks double as a series of raised terraces enclosed by a continuous wall of rough stabilised London Clay.

Chris Dercon Have you ever designed a private garden?

Günther Vogt I did, many years ago, but I don't do it anymore. Working for a private client is, for me, too intimate, and most of the private clients have seen so many things, they always want the same as everybody else.

Chris Dercon What did you intend by the title of your book *Landscape as a Cabinet of Curiosities*?

Günther Vogt We started with landscape as an attitude, but landscape is not an attitude in itself: it has to do with attitude. Our office in Zürich looks and feels like a cabinet of curiosities. Talking about a landscape attitude, think of the paintings of Turner, the photographs of Derek Jarman, the environments of Ian Hamilton Finlay, the way Western films narrate the symbolic differences between nature and gardens, and so on. My favourite film is *Dersu Uzala* (1975) by Akira Kurosawa. The Russian army sends an explorer on an expedition to the Siberian wilderness where he makes friends with a seasoned local hunter.

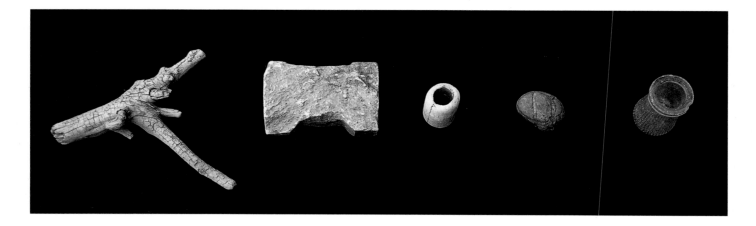

It's a film about what we can learn from nature and getting older. When you are walking through nature, like the explorer and the hunter in the film, you will find so many different things. Big and small. Complex and simple. What do you bring home? It's like organising a small exhibition: you're collecting, recollecting, recording and translating the things you've seen. Yet the arrangement of the cabinet of curiosities is not obvious. You have to invent and re-invent the order. So few people know anything about nature, landscape and plants anymore. The knowledge has disappeared in a dramatic way. Not so much in England, but in the rest of the world I really feel I cannot talk with as many people about what I'm doing. I've found out that I can do whatever I want. I can plant birch trees from the Himalayas and nobody will notice. Our distance from nature is growing, simply because plants do not grow everywhere any longer.

Chris Dercon Another book you have made is entitled *Miniature and Panorama*. Is the landscape or nature of Tate Modern a miniature or a panorama?

Günther Vogt It's both a miniature and a panorama, a model in reality.

End.

Jasper Morrison
in conversation with Chris Dercon

Chris Dercon Is this the first time that you've worked on such a large scale, for a museum?

Jasper Morrison The only time. It's the only time I've worked on anything architectural this big, yes. Herzog & de Meuron designed the built-in seating, but our brief was to design all the other furniture.

Chris Dercon What is your take on museums?

Jasper Morrison Take the V&A, for example, or any other museum that collects historical objects. They tend to collect the special ones, and not the everyday ones. The British Museum is perhaps an exception, because there you can find everyday objects from thousands of years ago. But I always find folk and ethno-logical museums more interesting. It's obvious why a museum would collect the more important things, but it's a pity that they ignore the everyday factor.

Chris Dercon But then, you're in trouble with contemporary art?

Jasper Morrison I don't talk about art. I think art is a completely different matter.

Chris Dercon In which kind of museum would you like to see your work, collected or put on display?

Jasper Morrison I suppose it would have to be a design museum. I mean, that's the reference – in as much as I try to design things that avoid messing themselves up with too much design, with an intention of too much design, so it's very difficult to put it in any other category. It is design, you know. It's done within the world of design.

Chris Dercon Are you an industrial designer?

Jasper Morrison I don't know if I would call myself an industrial designer. I think industrial designers concern themselves with more mechanical things. I'm probably a product designer, a furniture designer, which is what I studied. But I'm not a 'designer craftsman', or a 'limited edition designer artist'. I think I'm pretty much on the production side of design.

Chris Dercon So there might be an interesting confusion, then. People coming to Tate Modern and seeing these different chairs, and different configurations, might wonder if there has been one of those new artists at work who are interested in mimicking design.

Jasper Morrison Possibly. I'm trying to think which object would create confusion – perhaps the wooden benches.

Chris Dercon Because?

Jasper Morrison Because they're so reduced, so basic in shape.

<< Botan bench by Maruni, Japan Originally made in 2009, with a back, for the terrace of Jasper Morrison's office in Tokyo, it was then produced in cedar in 2013 by Maruni, who made a series of custom oak versions in different lengths for the Switch House in 2016.

> The Botan benches on level 2 of the Switch House.

Chris Dercon People might think they are minimal art!

Jasper Morrison They might, but I think they've got a bit too much character.

Chris Dercon Your furniture is often associated with minimal art.

Jasper Morrison I always hated being called a minimalist, and never understood why people did it.

Chris Dercon When did that start? The Thinking Man Chair in 1986 was not minimalist at all.

Jasper Morrison No, that's true. Perhaps after that. Would the Thinking Man's Chair work inside a museum?

Chris Dercon Yes.

Jasper Morrison I'm not sure. I think not.

Chris Dercon Why not?

Jasper Morrison I think the architects would object, for a start.

Chris Dercon Let's forget the architects.

Jasper Morrison I think the artists might even object. You know, it's a bit too strong. A bit too eye-catching. Not discreet enough. The kind of furniture we think of in museums and even art galleries is this kind of supportive, secondary-level, after the architecture, kind of 'We need something to sit on that won't disturb the atmosphere'. And I think the Thinking Man's Chair – although it has been used in certain art fairs – is a bit too much. I've always enjoyed the

Thinking Man's Chair
Painted steel
Cappellini, 1986.

atmosphere of galleries. And when I was a student I met people like Max Gordon – have you heard of him? He used to design a lot of galleries and was a fantastically clever guy because he picked what in many ways you could say is the most enjoyable and perhaps the easiest architectural project to do: a big empty space, avoiding all the hassle of a client's needs in their kitchen or their bathroom etc. I've always appreciated the atmosphere that you get in galleries, and I think even been inspired by it.

Chris Dercon Which spaces of Max Gordon spoke to you?

Jasper Morrison Well, the first Saatchi place. He did some galleries in Cork Street. He always got the work. He was the go-to guy.

Chris Dercon Don't you think these kinds of galleries look like … kind of generic? They all look the same? They are expressing a kind of domesticity yet they feel also corporate.

Jasper Morrison Yes. Perhaps that's why I found it inspiring, because it had this slightly domestic feel … I think in all of Max Gordon's places you'd say, 'Yes, this would make a great place to live'. The way I work is really about atmosphere.

Chris Dercon That's also the critique on these galleries, that they are almost too atmospheric.

Wooden furniture series designed for
Muji's domestic Japanese market in
2006.
A custom version of the chair with
an oiled finish was developed for
Tate in 2016.

Jasper Morrison I guess you have the same thing in design. You have the extremely neat and tidy ones, the Jonathan Ives, and you have the Studio Jobs, at the other end. I think they all have their place. It's no longer a world where we say, 'That's the only way to do it'.

Chris Dercon It's interesting that you use the term 'tidiness'. In your own work there is a tension between tidiness and a kind of normalness which is not tidy.

Jasper Morrison I know what you mean. There's always a moment when I ask myself, 'Does it look natural, or is it behaving naturally? Does it sit in the room in an unpretentious way, and will it therefore last? Will it maintain its character?' Because I think if a thing is not natural – if it's forced or overly tidied up, it won't last. It won't sit well in a space. I don't know whether the same applies for architecture. I suspect it's probably not the case. But the things you put into architecture, if they're not natural, they don't last.

Chris Dercon What makes things natural?

Jasper Morrison It could be something as banal as the angle of the back legs, or it could be too much expression. It could be, of course, colour and things like that. It's an intuition as well: it's looking at an object and saying, 'It doesn't look really right'. If I look at these chairs now [looking at the chairs in Chris Dercon's office] – the High-Pad chair (1998), I wonder if the flatness of the plywood on which the upholstery is put is really natural. Perhaps it would have been better if I could have got a bit more curve into it. But it was very early days, and we did things very quickly and, in a way, crudely then.

Chris Dercon 1998 – that's the beginning of your Super Normal [school] with Naoto Fukasawa.

Jasper Morrison Yes. In a way, though, it didn't have the name until 2006. The beginnings – the gropings for it. When I look at the chair now, it seems very flat-looking. It's still a useful chair, but it perhaps would have been more long-lasting with a bit more shape in the shell. So those are things that I might pick up on these days.

Chris Dercon Tate Modern is visited by millions of people. These millions are using the museum in quite a different way compared to the early days. They like to decide for themselves what they're doing in the museum. They consider the museum first and foremost as a place for encounters. How much does furniture influence their behaviour?

Jasper Morrison I've always enjoyed the conceit of design somehow creeping into those spaces, but remaining useful. I mean, not creeping into those spaces to show off, but to be useful. When I was at school, one of my great friends was the gallerist Paul Kasmin, and his father 'Kasmin' was a major Cork Street gallerist, so I grew up on the edge of this gallery world. I was very inspired by

the atmospheres that people in that world created for themselves, whether it was in the gallery or at home. There were people like David Hockney, Howard Hodgkin and Kasmin himself. The kind of interiors that those people occupied were very inspiring.

Chris Dercon They're like *Wunderkammers* – cabinets of curiosities – Pop-ish, or pop.

Jasper Morrison Yes. I think you're not born with an eye – you're born with the possibility of having one, and I think that the exposure to those kinds of people gave me my eye in a way.

Chris Dercon And the way these people lived, Kasmin and Max Gordon and David Hockney, is in contrast with today's collectors. There were a lot of possibilities to sit.

Jasper Morrison I think there's less possibility these days.

Chris Dercon I agree there's less possibility. I mean, when you see collectors' homes today, there is a lot of standing around, and it's almost like you walk into a gallery. It's almost embarrassing to sit. Because standing is a form of admiration, and sitting is probably something which is much more to do with yourself.

Jasper Morrison Yes. You've probably been to the Miró studio in Palma de Mallorca, designed by the architect Sert. There are an astonishing number of places to sit. Chairs of different sizes all over the studio.

Chris Dercon In Tate Modern there will be a lot of chairs as well. A lot of different chairs.

Jasper Morrison A place of that scale does need quite a few chairs. You think we've overdone it?

Chris Dercon People today request chairs again, they like to sit down. There is nothing more beautiful in a gallery than people leaning against walls, or finding a good corner. What would be an ideal bench for the Rothko room where the light levels are very low?

Jasper Morrison I think it should probably not have natural oak legs. It should rather be a much darker thing. If I think of a hard bench in a Rothko room, I think that's too much: you don't need to sit on a plank when you're looking at a Rothko. I think you need a bit of comfort. The Rothko paintings have a sort of blurred edge. I think if you sat on a hard bench you'd be disturbed by the contrast. You want something that will give a bit, to complement this kind of blurred edge effect. I remember a fantastic project Barry Flanagan did for museums in 1975, it was called the 'Rowford Process' – it was a series of very thin pieces of wood that were latticed. It was modular, maybe eighty by eighty centimetres, and you could put them together to make four or six, or three in a row, whatever you needed, but it was completely rigid. That was an interesting project. Completely the opposite of his hares with floppy ears. He even made a business card for it.

Chris Dercon It's interesting that you say that, these examples are in contrast to what you said before, that furniture should be a support act. Why didn't you propose to put chairs in the galleries?

Jasper Morrison It's perhaps partly conditioned by convention. But I think there may be good reasons why there are not chairs in museum spaces – although I always like the ones that are for the attendants.

HAL series of chairs designed for Vitra
between 2011 and 2015, with
a custom mix of wooden seats and
oak bases selected for Tate in 2016.

Chris Dercon Were you ever asked to design a chair for an attendant?

Jasper Morrison Not specifically, no.

Chris Dercon Would you like to do one?

Jasper Morrison I think it would be a strange project. I mean, they nearly always are chosen from a type of chair which is stacking, the quick set-up kind of chairs: light, easy to carry around. This might sound strange to use this word, but I think they are more seductive if they are chairs that come from another world. If it's designed specifically for the gallery, for the guard to sit on, it could be a bit too much. It might make the atmosphere too formal, even pretentious.

Chris Dercon What do you mean by 'a bit too much'?

Jasper Morrison I don't know. I suddenly have images of a type of private collection museum, where the collector has commissioned someone to design the chair that the guard will sit on. It's like nothing has been allowed in from the outside world. It kind of doesn't work. Even when architects design their own chairs – like Oscar Niemeyer for the Communist headquarters in Paris – they're completely crazy chairs, and they kind of fit well. But on the other hand there's something a bit too contained when no germs are allowed to get in. I think you need to allow a bit of outside in. It would be too much if everything in the Tate was designed especially for the Tate. It's kind of more fun if it's a bit of a mix. Whereas going to a real extreme, where the architect designs everything for the museum, including all the furniture, I think there'd be a lack of tension, there'd be no play between seeing something that you recognise as a normal piece of equipment from the world and a new building. It helps the new building a lot, because it puts it in context. Let's not forget, as the furniture is there to serve, so is the architecture. In the end, they're serving the art.

Chris Dercon Or they are serving the audience.

Jasper Morrison Good point! Again, I come back to that word 'naturalness'. It's a question of naturalness, and it's pretty unnatural to have a room where everything is designed in one way, or from one hand.

Chris Dercon Is that also why you question uniformity? At Tate we have many different types of furniture. You like mixing different types of furniture. Has that also to do with naturalness?

Jasper Morrison Partly, I mean, one of the most interesting aspects of the Tate job is understanding how specific the needs are, from one part of the building to another. In some cases there are no products on the market which do what you need them to do. Like the tables in the restaurant which have to be folded and put away. You have a fairly small storage space, and you have a lot of tables, and they need to be folded very quickly and taken away, almost every day. We've developed this table that folds – it's called the Super-Fold. There's a lever under the top: you pull the lever and slightly lift the top, and as the top folds vertically, parallel to the column, the base lifts up and rotates into the same line. So in the end, you end up with a very flat table which can be stored.

Chris Dercon You're talking like an industrial designer.

Jasper Morrison Almost! Going back to the diversity of the furniture, it's really a function of what you need in different places, that's just the reality. One chair wouldn't do the job.

Chris Dercon How important is it to be able to carry furniture around? Or, are you happy with the fact that furniture sits in one place?

Jasper Morrison I think chairs are better off when you can actually lift them and move them around. On the other hand, the reality is, once a table is put in place, it doesn't get moved very much. In public spaces though, you might actually need something that can't be moved.

Chris Dercon You are not at all afraid of mixing the old and the new.

Jasper Morrison No, I think that's great fun. I once put together an exhibition at the Musée des Arts Décoratifs in Bordeaux – to find objects that are so complementary that even though there might be 300 years between them, in some cases people would not even notice.

Chris Dercon Did it ever occur to you to take older types and insert them in your newer work, and look back retrospectively and say, 'Something which I did in 1998 might be very interesting, twenty years later almost, to mix it with things I'm doing today'? Is that something common, in furniture design, to look back and to bring things back – to go back and forth?

Jasper Morrison No, not really.

Chris Dercon Why not?

Jasper Morrison I don't know why not.

Chris Dercon But you do it sometimes.

Jasper Morrison I do it to some extent. Some old furniture works better to be mixed with new furniture than others. I mean, you can take a lot of the Danish design by people like Børge Mogensen and it still looks fantastic. Maybe it looks better than it did fifty years ago.

Chris Dercon You and some of your colleagues, Hella Jongerius and Konstantin Grcic, are not shying away from using upholstery and textiles.

Jasper Morrison The new textiles coming out are just amazing.

Chris Dercon Why are they so amazing?

Jasper Morrison They bring so much life. If you look at older fabrics like 'Hopsack', the one that was used on the Eames aluminium chairs, it's a very

worthy woven wool, but flat as a pancake. Totally different from the look and feel of the more technical fabrics that are coming from companies like Kvadrat today, which have so much depth and so much sympathy with other materials like wood and stainless steel. You could use those fabrics and put them on old designs and they would look completely new again. It's the power of fabrics today: so much colour and richness which wasn't there before, which wasn't on offer. And maybe we're all a bit braver. I think in the past you would struggle to find a new fabric, for a new design. The manufacturer would say, 'This is our standard collection – choose one of these'.

Chris Dercon The furniture for Tate Modern has a lot of colour as well.

Jasper Morrison In the lounges.

Chris Dercon How important is colour?

Jasper Morrison The colours of these new fabrics which are coming out are so much more subtle than they used to be, and perhaps so well considered as a collection that you can mix them together and achieve something much more interesting and successful than you could in the past. And again the performance of the fabrics is so much better than it used to be.

Chris Dercon The Super Normal school with Naoto Fukasawa, how far is that away for you? Where are we now?

Jasper Morrison I still think that one of the most important things for design to do for itself and others, as a favour, would be to get a little bit closer to normal everyday life, and not to be seen as the centrepiece on the table to give people something to talk about. There's a dislocation between what people perceive as something they'll put in their house, and 'Design', which they think of as something to encounter in restaurants, or in museums. I think that we need to get the two together again.

When you look at the history of the household thing, people would go out and a buy a chair made by the guy at the end of the street. You know, that was a more real situation than the one we have today, where we're designing these kinds of fantasy objects to attract attention, to fish for customers. But it fails because we're not doing things that are perceived as normal or even everyday options for people. People themselves don't buy that stuff, because it's over-designed. Too much of a statement. So that's my interest. I still think of Super Normal as a way to close that gap. Design could go a bit closer to being stuff that people use without too much nonsense. If you make a cup of tea, does there need to be a conversation about the teapot? Or isn't it nicer that the teapot contributes to the atmosphere in a positive way, without demanding to be noticed? Think of Philippe Starck's lemon squeezer, there's no way in the world that somebody could avoid having a conversation about it while using one! I'm aware that they've sold millions of them but isn't that completely the wrong way of thinking about objects? I feel that most 'Design' stuff is worse than non-designers' stuff in terms of satisfying an everyday atmosphere. It's over-expressive, it's awkward, it's unnatural, it doesn't last very long, visually. Perhaps it's even a misconception of the role of design – where design becomes a form of entertainment rather than a form of practicality.

Chris Dercon Does that also mean that the museum has to think twice, when it offers merchandise in the museum shop?

Jasper Morrison I would agree with you there. Museum shops can for me sometimes be the killer – the least sexy part of the visit. I've been through the galleries, seen wonderful things, I feel that the world is new and bright, and then I come through the shop and find it's full of junk, which brings me down to earth with a bump. Wouldn't it be fantastic if the museum bookshop could be run by a second-hand book dealer, or have an element of that? I personally find that rows of newly published art books are not really doing the trick.

Chris Dercon Do you consider yourself a British designer?

Jasper Morrison No, not so much. I think I've broken that bond, in a professional sense – I mean, not in a personal sense. I still feel very British and living abroad you become more British than if you'd stayed behind. I'm not even sure what British design is, although I would say my work is quite British. There's a certain dry, restrained sense of humour, completely allergic to ostentation, which I admire in the British, and try to stay true to in designing things.

Chris Dercon Your furniture is never ironical or cynical, unlike Marcel Wanders or Studio Job.

Jasper Morrison Not too cynical. I'm not into that. The more you travel the more important your background becomes in a way. I think every European culture has something to offer, I mean, some more than others. I'd say Italy, Denmark and Switzerland are amazing. I've taken so much from all of them. And I always wondered, when I was in Berlin in the early 1980s, when I was learning so much from the German Werkbund and Dieter Rams, why German designers were ignoring these 'roots'.

Chris Dercon How important is Germany for you, or Switzerland?

Jasper Morrison Both are very important. I don't know if you know that I had a scholarship in Berlin in '83, '84 – something called the Shakespeare Scholarship.

Chris Dercon No clue! I thought it was a DAAD scholarship.

Jasper Morrison That was later, that was '88. Yes, Hochschule der Künste, HDK was where I studied. The Shakespeare Prize was awarded to an artist by

a Hamburg benefactor with a certain amount of money. So David Hockney
was awarded that prize in '83, I think, and he had to choose someone for
the Scholarship. He didn't have any idea who to give it to, and Kasmin said,
'Why don't you give it to Jasper?' And –

Chris Dercon   So you were the prize student to Hockney!

Jasper Morrison   Yes, so I was shipped off to Berlin. Actually, I could have chosen
anywhere, but I chose Berlin. I had a friend who was teaching there, at the HDK,
so it was much easier to do it that way. So my middle year of Royal College I spent
in Berlin, which was fantastic. I was obsessed by all the Behrens buildings and
I went to find them all, took photos of them and the Werkbund …

Chris Dercon   Back to Britain. Are there still makers here?

Jasper Morrison   No. I think it's a disaster. I felt it going after leaving the Royal
College in 1986. Margaret Thatcher was busy driving out every workshop,
stubbing out every last ember of specialist making workshops. The rents were
going up, and all the workshops that were in London were disappearing, and
now I think there's no skill left, not much anyway.

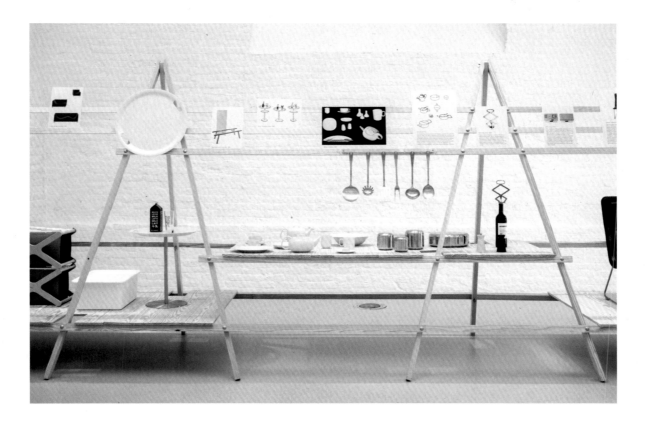

Chris Dercon Nothing?

Jasper Morrison It became a dirty idea that you would want to make anything. I mean, perhaps I'm giving Thatcher too much of the blame, but she certainly contributed strongly, and I think we just lost the plot. We've lost the skill.

Chris Dercon And what's the role of Tate Modern in all of this?

Jasper Morrison I think it's really important to have these kinds of anchors in London. When you come in on the train from Gatwick, before you cross the river, the Tate comes into your mind – whether you see it or you don't see it, you're aware of something good being there, it's reassuring.

Chris Dercon Reassuring in which sense?

Jasper Morrison In the sense of being in London – a city with those sorts of cultural institutions makes you feel good about the city, a city without is a very poor place to be. Tate is counterweight against all the crap that goes on in government. All the wasted money, all the stupid ideas, all the dumb wars. It's a kind of public compensation for all that nonsense.

Chris Dercon Talking about nonsense, what is your association with the term 'creative industries' invented by Labour?

Jasper Morrison Yes – bullshit. I mean you know that Britain is the only EU member that allows designs to be copied and copies of design to be sold? It's basically the back door to Europe for all those businesses that reproduce designs illegally and sell them. There's no visual culture in government, in British government. Luckily, we still have the Tate!

End.

The original Post-it note diagram created in 2010 to describe the new Tate Modern in a simple and instantly readable form. The diagram shows the relationship of the galleries, education spaces and social spaces, either side of the Turbine Hall and reveals the 'circular art route'.

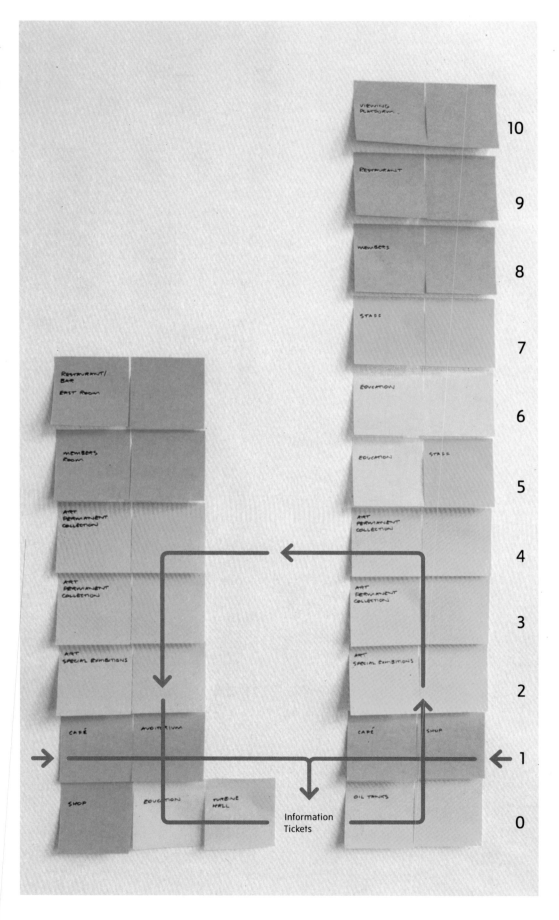

Ian Cartlidge
in conversation with
Chris Dercon

Chris Dercon What's your role?

Ian Cartlidge Tate Modern will offer a very different visitor experience when the new building opens in 2016. Our role, as wayfinding designers, is to ensure that visitors understand the new space, feel welcome and well informed and can navigate the whole building and its contents easily.

We work closely with the architects to achieve this. Visitor flow is fundamental to the architectural concept. Herzog & de Meuron have designed a scheme that carefully considers how visitors interact with the space: how they behave in different environments. For example, the transition from intimate space to voluminous, the reading of light and shade, the impact of sight lines etc. Our job is to enhance the visitors' understanding of these natural cues that exist in the architecture and add a layer of graphic information that contributes to the making of a coherent building and a positive visitor experience.

Herzog & de Meuron haven't simply continued the original architectural language out into the south landscape, they have built something entirely new and different; and yet it has a really strong connection to the original building. There is a striking difference of form on the outside, but from within it's actually quite difficult to see where one starts and the other one ends.

Chris Dercon That's also a problem for your work.

Ian Cartlidge Fundamental to our thinking is considering how visitors perceive the space from within. A very important part of the brief was about 'single entity'. The new building and the existing building should feel seamless from within. The scheme hasn't been designed as an existing building with an extension – it is very much a completion of a grand plan and there are natural connections between the two spaces that feel like they have been 'revealed' rather than 'created' from scratch. The buildings have to flow into each other naturally, and this is what Herzog & de Meuron have achieved; we are simply reinforcing this with our graphic interventions.

Chris Dercon Your contribution is about wayfinding. At the new Tate Modern, there are multiple entrances. So what do you do?

Ian Cartlidge Yes, we have to deal with multiple entrances – of course the arrival experience is crucial in forming coherence and visitor confidence at the start of the journey and the new building will have a big impact on the arrival experience, especially on level 1.

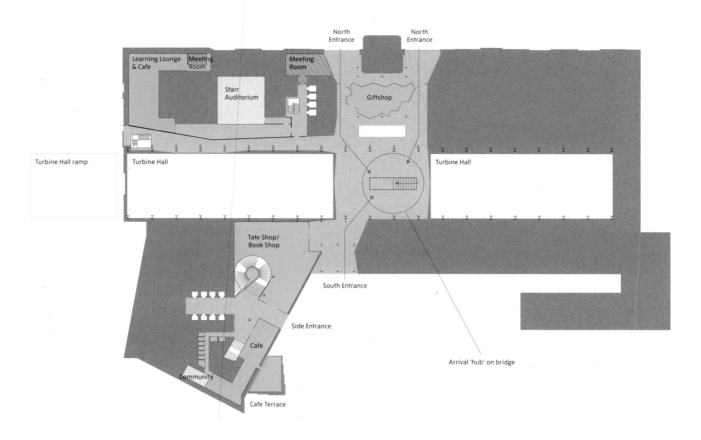

The original Tate Modern scheme, opened in 2000, envisaged the west entrance as the Main entrance. Entering at this point, you experience the grand arrival in the vast Turbine Hall which reveals the size and shape of the building. Everything makes sense from this approach and you begin to form a mental model of the space. You are gently led to the bottom of the ramp where you naturally arrive at the ticket and Information desk. Behind the glazed wall to your left is the lift core and the dramatic escalators which take you directly to the galleries on level 2 – this is the perfect place to start your visit to Tate Modern. But, of course, visitors decide, over time, where they want to enter.

Chris Dercon Did you see a shift?

Ian Cartlidge Yes, the success of Tate Modern accelerated the development and popularity of Bankside and the footfall along the river increased to levels way beyond those imagined. This resulted in the River entrance becoming the most popular entrance. Prior to the opening of the new building, eighty percent of visitors entered Tate Modern via the River entrance.

Entering via the River entrance on level 1 was less intuitive than entering via the West entrance on level 0. There isn't the same sense of arrival and visitors need to work harder to orientate. Visitors quickly found themselves on the Turbine Hall Bridge which was a dead-end space with seemingly little purpose.

With the opening of the new building, the arrival experience on level 1 changes dramatically and this is key to improving the wayfinding via the River entrance. It now has an equivalent sense of arrival as that experienced at the west entrance. By opening up a new entrance to the south, Herzog & de Meuron have effectively created 'a street' running across the Turbine Hall from north to

< A diagram showing the level 1 arrival principle. The new south entrance has created a 'street' running through the Turbine Hall. The bridge, which used to be a dead end space, now becomes an 'arrival hub' at the heart of the building. The stairs in the Turbine Hall Bridge pull visitors down to level 0 where they find the main information and ticket desk and can clearly see the Switch House and Boiler House entrances on either side – the perfect place to start their visit.

> The relationship of the galleries arranged either side of the Turbine Hall is evident and the circular art route is shown as the primary artery running through the building.

∨ An early sketch exploring the relationship of the key building components and the flow between the two sides of the Turbine Hall.

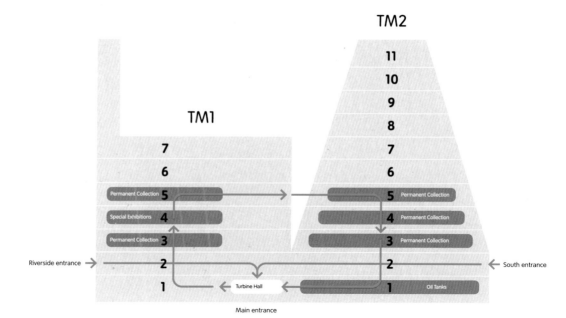

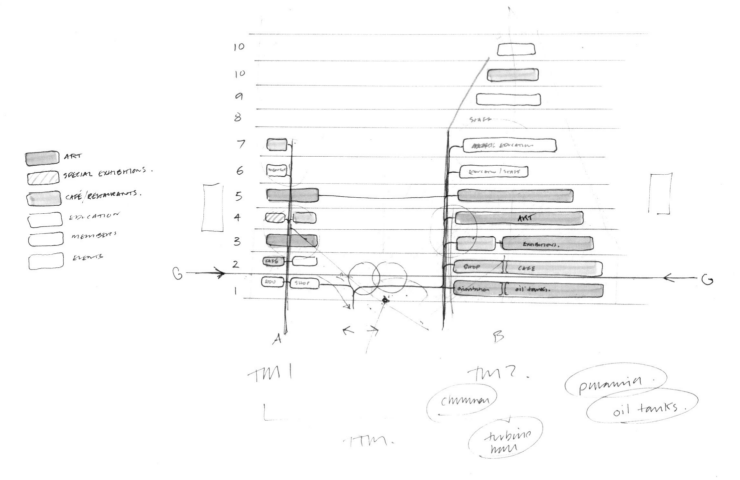

south on level 1. Visitors will be naturally drawn onto the centre of the Turbine Hall bridge which will now feel like the 'heart of the building' with activity visible on either side. Visitors will be able to read the building from this new central point. They will get a sense of its shape and layout and begin to develop a mental model of the space. This will be a great place to congregate, plan your first move and start your visit to Tate Modern. The Turbine Hall Bridge, with openings to the landscape either side, will feel like an extension to Bankside's public realm. Visitors will be drawn into this space on the bridge through the intimate scale thresholds, and the transition into the light and voluminous space of the Turbine Hall will create a dramatic sense of arrival.

Chris Dercon Günther Vogt was saying that the experience of Tate Modern starts outside.

Ian Cartlidge It is true that the iconic building, which can be seen from a great distance across the river, and the generous landscape in front begin the process of anticipation and sense of arrival even before you enter the site. The wayfinding elements such as the banners and entrance graphics play an important role here in communicating the vibrancy and diversity of what's happening inside. This reassures visitors who have come to see a specific exhibition and it also draws visitors in who are passing by or simply enjoying the landscape; the visit experience really does start outside. This will become even stronger with the introduction of the new south entrance and southern landscape and the connection through the building between the two.

So the external and internal experiences are inextricably linked. The new south entrance is key to completing the balance of circulation and sense of arrival on level 1; it will feel like it was always there. Orientation will feel more

The arrival experience on level 1 has changed dramatically with the opening of the new south entrance. When entering at the River entrance, the daylight visible at the opposite side of the building naturally draws visitors onto the Turbine Hall Bridge where they can orientate. It has become a new civic space where visitors can congregate and plan their first move.

natural and you will be able to understand the building from all entrances. It feels like the building has been waiting for its moment.

Chris Dercon   What's the next problem to solve?

Ian Cartlidge   Developing a quick understanding of the building and its contents on arrival is key to achieving coherence at the start of the journey. At the very beginning of the project we explored how to communicate the new 'single entity' building to visitors in a simple and instantly readable form. We created a simple 'Post-It note diagram' which showed the levels of the building, stacked either side of the Turbine Hall and how they connect with each other. We colour coded the diagram which immediately revealed the logical arrangement of the building with the galleries aligned across the Turbine Hall on levels 2, 3 and 4.

The 'street' running through the building on level 1 and the addition of the level 4 Turbine Hall bridge have created the idea of a circular 'art flow' through the building. This circular art route is central to the building layout. All the other facilities, such as the learning and social spaces, are located either above or below so you can perceive the building as having art at the centre with other spaces off this central core.

Our 'Post-It note diagram' formed the basis of the 'brick wayfinding diagram' that you see in the building today. This is a level directory that orientates you horizontally as well as vertically. It places you in the building and informs your next move. It is a schematic cross-section of the building which enables visitors to form a quick mental model of the building and how the spaces connect.

Chris Dercon   Do you tell visitors that Tate Modern is showing the collection in a very different way and also offers many different exhibitions?

Ian Cartlidge   Yes. There is a wide diversity of experience on offer at Tate Modern which we need to communicate. There are also many different visitor types – some people want to immerse themselves in the art experience; other visitors may want the art experience to play a relatively small part in their visit because they've come to socialise, to enjoy the space. So yes, we have to deal with the diversity of what's on offer and the diversity of visitor types. We have to communicate to all of them very clearly and provide information that tells them what's on and how to find it, so then they can make their own choice and decide how they want to visit Tate Modern.

This process starts at the entrance thresholds where we have designed a series of fly-posters – a design language adopted from the street, reinforcing the notion of the landscape flowing through the building. These posters present the diversity on offer at Tate Modern – a diversity which is increasing with the extended space. You encounter the posters as you step inside the building, and you get a sense that here there are exhibitions, displays, events, films, learning experiences and, of course, shopping, eating and drinking. You can also see what is free and what is paid for. So this is very important information for the visitor at the start of their journey.

Chris Dercon What you're doing is always coming back to communication.

Ian Cartlidge Everything we do is about communication; whether we are designing printed material, a website or wayfinding, it's all about how people navigate their way through information, how they filter information and make decisions.

Herzog & de Meuron are also communicating to the visitor through their architecture. Visitors will take their orientation cues as much from the building layout, landmarks, surface textures, light, colour etc. as they do from signage and information graphics. Signage is only one tool, within the set of tools that we utilise for wayfinding. For example, when entering on level 1, visitors will be drawn onto the level 1 bridge because the light from the south and the volume of the Turbine Hall will pull them through the more intimate threshold spaces – this is a very theatrical experience, it creates anticipation and a sense of arrival – it's all carefully considered as well as ultimately intuitive. Our job is to enhance the intuitive experience by adding a layer of communication consisting of signage, information graphics, colour and terminology.

Chris Dercon I found it very amusing how you played with semantics.

Ian Cartlidge Well, terminology is very important in wayfinding, because it is a big point of reference for visitors. People like to be able to form a mental map of a space and terminology helps with this process. The new Tate Modern requires names to describe the two primary spaces either side of the Turbine Hall to assist flow between them.

We decided to reinforce the legacy of the power station by naming these spaces after their historical usage: Boiler House and Switch House. These names join the established power station terminology of Turbine Hall and The Tanks. This makes it very specific to Tate Modern. It also establishes the building as one; you now have two equivalent spaces to either side of the Turbine Hall, not an existing building with a new extension. People will inevitably refer to the 'new building' initially, but we are thinking long-term; it won't be the new building forever. This gets back to the notion that Tate Modern, old and new, is a single entity.

Chris Dercon Are there further tools?

Ian Cartlidge Yes, graphic language is an integral part of achieving effective wayfinding. Not only in the sense of clarity and legibility but also in terms of design aesthetics and appropriateness. We have designed a graphic language that is integrated with the architecture. It is designed to feel as if it is part of the building fabric, not added on at a later date. This makes the wayfinding more powerful and believable for the visitor, and places it in the context: belonging to the architecture, not a brand overlay.

We have achieved this by devising a palette of materials and techniques that are applied directly to the surfaces of the building: painted lettering, fly-posters, projected lettering and heat-applied vinyl – they all touch the surfaces of the building in a manner which allows the contours of the walls to show through. So when we apply fly-posters to a raw, rough surface such as the concrete walls in the Tanks, the texture becomes part of the poster and graphic and wall become 'as one'.

What we're not doing is applying panels onto the building, such as metal, square signs or raised letters. These would look 'added' and not be specific to the building. Only the donor recognition, which is a distinct layer of information, uses metal panels and these are cast which gives them a strong connection with the industrial past of the building.

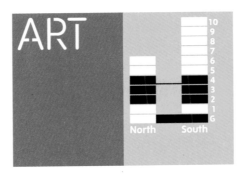
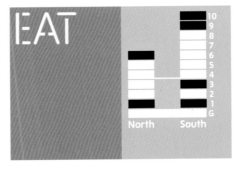
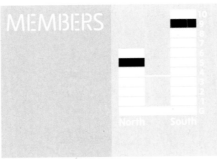
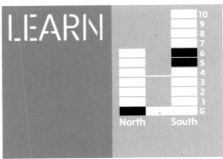

Chris Dercon But that's a dangerous area. You never got into a conflict with the architects? The architect Stephan Braunfels notoriously said 'no' to having anything on or near his Pinakothek der Moderne in Munich.

Ian Cartlidge Herzog & de Meuron recognise the importance of information and graphic intervention in a public building such as Tate Modern. We are all working towards a common goal: visitor communication. Our graphic interventions are carefully considered, not only in the context of visitor movement but also in the context of the architecture. Yet our graphic language is not over-respectful of the building. It's got a presence of its own; it has impact, because this is what visitors need.

Chris Dercon But not just an impact, you create also intimacy and even domesticity.

Ian Cartlidge Well it's not a corporate approach, which is very uniform, very consistent, very didactic, very unforgiving. By integrating with the architecture we create a warmth and a human quality.

Chris Dercon One with authority.

Ian Cartlidge The authority comes from the design language we have developed. Visitors believe information that appears integrated, they don't believe information if it looks 'stuck-on' or temporary.

Chris Dercon What about the font?

Ian Cartlidge We have used the font that was originally designed for Tate in 2000 by Wolff Olins. This font is firmly established as part of Tate's brand.

What we have done is develop a sub-brand for Tate Modern by refreshing the typographic identity. We introduced the thin version of the font which was little used previously. 'Tate New Pro Thin' has a contemporary feel yet it is also timeless. We introduced capital letters for headings and retuned the typographic language to suit Tate Modern's content and architecture.

Chris Dercon You're using the word 'brand'. I read somewhere that you don't like the word, the term 'brand'.

Ian Cartlidge No.

Chris Dercon Why not?

Ian Cartlidge I think the term brand can be too corporate, especially for a museum. It can be too prescriptive. I prefer the term 'visual language', or 'visual identity'. Brand speaks of big, heavy, corporate organisations, an authoritarian vocabulary, this is not the direction museums are heading in.

Chris Dercon How would you describe in a few sentences, the visual identity of Tate and of Tate Modern? Some people say Tate Modern is an art movement by itself – and that it stands for much more than art. It should also stand for public domain and publicness.

Projection and fly-posting lends itself
well to the raw spaces in the Tanks.

Ian Cartlidge I feel that the visual identity of Tate Modern is very connected to the art. It is a contemporary visual language appropriate to its subject, but importantly, it has a timeless quality: it isn't fashionable for the sake of being fashionable. It has consistency across a wide range of applications and this speaks of a large organisation, but it does not attempt to be bigger than the art – this is a very important balance to strike.

The publicness of Tate Modern is determined by its scale and the wide range of experience it offers. The Turbine Hall is becoming an extension of London's public realm. Tate Modern is becoming much more than an art gallery – it is bigger than that, it has great social spaces, common areas where people meet, socialise or just hang out. It has cafés and restaurants, a bar, learning spaces and shopping; but all these things have art at their core and this is reflected in the visual identity.

Chris Dercon At the same time there is a feeling of belonging. It gives also a sense of 'I feel at home here'.

Ian Cartlidge Yes, I think that's true.

Chris Dercon Because nobody's telling me what to do.

Ian Cartlidge Exactly. Firstly we have to strike a careful balance; we have to provide enough information to the visitor but not overload them with information. Visitors should feel informed but not uncomfortably so; we want to give them enough information to enable them to decide what they want to do and how they want to do it. Then the tone of voice in which this is communicated is crucial; not shouting, but clear and impactful and, importantly, there when you need it.

Chris Dercon A visit to Tate Modern is like luxury of choice: namely, I can decide for myself where to go, what to do, and for how long, what I want to think about, if I want to buy something or not …

Ian Cartlidge I compare visiting Tate Modern to visiting a district within a city. There are many ways you can explore that district, many experiences you can have and many ways you can enter and exit. It isn't a small building where you enter one way and follow a particular route – you have a choice. And that is one of the unique things about the space. What we have to do as wayfinding designers is to ensure that visitors have the right information, at the right time in their journey, to enable them to make decisions about what to do or what to see, but not to over-sign. Over-signing encroaches on the visitor experience in a negative way.

Chris Dercon There are new wayfinding tools, coming from digital technologies. You have started to use 'projections'.

Ian Cartlidge We have used projections in the Tanks for the headline art programme, but this isn't digital projection, they are gobo projectors like those used in a theatre with static imagery. This is one of our 'direct to surface' design language techniques.

Digital technology will have an increasingly important role to play in the visitor experience. However, we don't want to over-digitise the visitor information; on-site, it has to find its place in the overall information system. We have developed an analogue approach to information on-site; for example, no digital screens for programme content, just low-tech, fly-posters which convey this information very well.

You have to be very careful when considering digital displays in public buildings as they can create unwanted dwell points. It's difficult for more than two or three visitors to look at a screen at any one time, so it's quite an individual experience. If we do introduce screens in the future, perhaps because of further programme expansion, they will be in spaces where people can stand back and look at them collectively.

Chris Dercon Like in the airport.

Ian Cartlidge Like in the airport, yes. But again it's a balance, and the last thing we want to do is make Tate Modern feel like an airport – the majority of signage within the building will always be low-tech: painted, fly-posted, projected etc.

Chris Dercon Now, young people will say, 'I don't want to look at these big signs – I'd rather use my phone'.

Ian Cartlidge This is true. The digital experience will play an important part off-site, in the form of the website and in the future as part of the visitor experience on-site, on visitors' own mobile devices. This is the future of wayfinding: giving visitors the choice of how to navigate; giving them their own private digital experience as an extra layer to the physical wayfinding embedded in the architecture.

GPS apps, accessed on hand-held devices, are becoming part of the public building wayfinding experience – it's happening. But what's important is that the information you have on your smartphone has a relationship to the information you encounter in the physical world. These two worlds will co-exist and should work intelligently together.

Chris Dercon The banners, as Vogt is saying, are the modern translation of an old-fashioned idea.

Ian Cartlidge The banners have an established relationship to the external environment. They flap around in the wind and there is something about their scale. They are visible from a distance and let you know what's happening within the building. One of the strengths of Tate Modern's location is its river frontage, and this is a great place for banners to help create a sense of arrival. The journey really does begin in the landscape at Tate Modern. This is the external threshold. There is a strong connection to the river with a lot of space between the river and the entrance to the building. The banners on the site perimeter define this space, they tell you that you have entered and your experience has begun. It is exactly the same on the south side, with a generous new landscape; the banners mark the site perimeter and the space between the banners and the entrance is where the visit experience begins.

When you approach from the south, you get a glimpse of the new building from Southwark Street – it's a narrow view framed by the glass buildings on either side of the road, but you get a glimpse of the tower. As the tower is revealed, next you see the chimney of the existing building – and then you notice the banners. The banners' job is to pull you to the right point at which to enter the landscape.

There are also prominent circular walls on the south perimeter, circumscribing the contours of the tanks below. We have intentionally kept these relatively neutral because we want to make them disappear into the landscape and allow the building to draw people towards it.

Chris Dercon Tate Modern is surrounded by glass architecture, by corporate architecture and hyper-expensive residencies, many of which are unoccupied. How do you express the difference with Tate: 'We are different – we are not corporate'?

Ian Cartlidge Well, I think it's a striking contrast. This is what I really love about Herzog & de Meuron's approach, because they've gone in completely the opposite direction to all of that. In a way, it makes these other buildings look even more corporate, because the Tate Modern architecture – the twisted form of the tower, the brick cladding and the asymmetric arrangement of the openings – contrasts so well against these surrounding archetypal corporate buildings.

Chris Dercon What is your association with the twisted form, the folds, of the new tower?

Ian Cartlidge It isn't just one form: you've seen one elevation, you've seen them all. Instead, you get a different experience from each approach. And this for me adds to the experience of your visit. I think Tate Modern is one of the few art museums in the world where the visual experience of the architecture adds to the experience of the art in such a powerful and relevant way. The word 'fold' describes the form of the tower very well.

Chris Dercon What do you associate the word 'fold' with?

Ian Cartlidge The 'unexpected'.

Chris Dercon Architectural historian Mark Wigley said during a talk at the last Venice Architecture Biennale: 'Museums should be embracing the strangeness and complexity of the relationship between ourselves and a work of art'. 'We don't need,' says Wigley, 'a simple image of a museum to pretend that everything is straightforward.'

Ian Cartlidge Well, in this sense the new Tate Modern building is a perfect illustration. Nothing is straightforward with the architectural image. On one hand it has a familiar presence, the brick cladding blending into the original power station, the tower echoing the height of the chimney; but it is also unexpected and surprising. From some viewpoints the folded elevations seem impossible, as if the building is defying the laws of gravity. This initial, exciting encounter with the building attunes you to the experience you are about to have inside the building; it's the prelude to your visit and it creates a dramatic sense of arrival.

Chris Dercon The job for Tate Modern was simple compared to what you had to do for and in the Barbican …

Ian Cartlidge The Barbican was also a collaboration with Studio Myerscough and we are both fans of that building. The original Arts Centre designed by Chamberlain, Powell and Bon was well designed, and a very good example of brutalist architecture of the period – in some ways surpassing the National Theatre in my opinion. However, due to many disrupting factors, the design and construction work took a very long time from concept to realisation, and the management of the Arts Centre at the time of opening decided that the new way forward was the Lloyds Building which was just being unveiled down the road and this brutalist concrete approach was already out of fashion.

They perceived the building as a concrete labyrinth out of step with the times, so they decided on a series of entirely inappropriate interventions such as murals, bad carpet decisions and lighting. This rendered the building illegible and it had the result of making it very confused. One of the first things that we did when we took the project on was strip back the clutter and reveal the original building, and immediately it became more readable as a space.

There were some flaws with the arrangement of the space, of course, which needed to be addressed, and the architects Allford Hall Monaghan Morris made the circulation and the reading of the building more intuitive through a series of sensitive architectural interventions. Like Tate Modern, we worked closely with the architects to develop a totally integrated wayfinding scheme.

Chris Dercon You worked for the *Guardian*. Is there a connection with the new Tate Modern? Some compare the new functions, such as Tate Exchange, the meeting places, the concourses and lounges, with concepts of new offices – such as the *Guardian* – which are becoming more like spaces for encounters, whereby often the distinction between producers and receivers gets blurred.

164

Ian Cartlidge Absolutely. There is a connection with the *Guardian*. The way the culture of an office like the *Guardian* works – it's about providing social spaces for interaction and conversation, and that's where things happen, not necessarily at your desk. And Tate Modern has these wonderful, common spaces where you can congregate and meet; it's not an office but the principle is the same – you can pause and reflect in these shared spaces. This happens in the Turbine Hall now – you see people sitting on the floor and you see people in the concourses, which are wonderful places for people to meet, sit, pause and reflect. The new concourses are going to provide even more of these common spaces, exciting spaces where encounters and conversation can happen – it's a very important part of the experience.

Chris Dercon Lots of seats.

Ian Cartlidge Lots of seats – a great range of furniture by Jasper Morrison, as well as the built-in furniture designed by Herzog & de Meuron that's carefully positioned in pockets of space so as not to interrupt flow. Posters will be placed in these areas to position information at dwell points where people have time to read it. There will also be seating built into the architecture – the deep, angled window reveals in the new building are effectively seats; it will be great to see these spaces occupied. And I'm sure people will sit on the floor in the new building too. This is where conversation will happen. It's very much about the relationship between social spaces and art spaces – these divisions will be blurred, it will be one, unique Tate Modern experience.

Chris Dercon Tate Modern is even reflecting the work you have been doing in Selfridges. Tate also has things for sale.

Ian Cartlidge Of course, the retail and the catering at Tate Modern are an integral part of the experience, they are very important. Selfridges, in parts, aspires to be a gallery, to create the atmosphere of an exhibition where the display is for sale – there is an interesting comparison here.

Visitors can engage with Tate Modern in many different ways; they can eat, drink and, yes, go shopping. This translates into revenue, a percentage of which feeds directly back into the art, so it's a circle. Art is at the core of Tate Modern, but it's very important that we drive people to these places too.

Chris Dercon How do you do that?

Ian Cartlidge Well, what we don't do is over-sign; we do it by making visitors aware of the diversity on offer and allowing them to make a choice. Again the architecture plays a big role in the positioning of shops: you are never far away from a shop and you will come across them naturally in your journey, so we don't overstate it with the wayfinding.

Fly-posting, painting and heat-applied vinyl, which are material techniques established in The Tanks, on level 0, are pulled-up through the building to the more refined upper level concourses in the Switch House. Wayfinding information is positioned in consistent locations on each level.

Chris Dercon What's next?

> **Ian Cartlidge** We enjoy working in the cultural sector. We are currently working on the wayfinding and signage for the new Design Museum in London and the Musée d'Art de Nantes. We particularly enjoy working with interesting client teams and architects where the working relationship is an enjoyable and rewarding one – this is where great work happens, the process is almost as important as the end result. The journey that we've had on the Tate Modern project is a great example of this – a fully integrated scheme where all design disciplines have worked closely together. You can feel this in the end result.

Chris Dercon Which type of architects do you prefer?

> **Ian Cartlidge** We have to remember that the architect is not our client. Tate Modern is our client, or the Barbican, or the *Guardian*. But these spaces are built by architects and we enjoy being part of an integrated design team to fully realise the finished building – it's a combined effort. I sometimes compare wayfinding with other integral design services which contribute to the finished building, such as structural engineering; the building won't be as effective

without it and good clients and architects recognise this. So we like architects where this relationship can happen. We have enjoyed many such fruitful collaborations.

Chris Dercon   Which schools of graphic design did you take your inspiration from?

Ian Cartlidge   In our formative years we looked towards Europe and in particular the Dutchman Wim Crouwel and his company Total Design. I think it's the modernity of the work. In the seventies, when they were working at their peak, it was new, it was refreshing, it was modern, it was cutting through something that was there, and that made it exciting. It was like the future, in a way. We don't slavishly follow that specific design school, but the Dutch approach is in our roots. Of course the Swiss influence is strong too and artists such as Lawrence Weiner and Ed Ruscha are important points of reference. If you think wayfinding, then Ulm is a big influence as well.

Chris Dercon   When you look at the issues museums will have to deal with in the future, such as slow engagement or slow experience, how can you contribute to slowing down things?

Ian Cartlidge   This can be done by careful placement of information and giving consideration to how much information you use. You have to give people space between their decision-making points in a journey – to give them a feeling of freedom. Rather than imposing prescriptive routing.

You need to develop a wayfinding strategy to allow visitors to have freedom, but not to feel that they're alone in their journey. You need to make visitors feel that they have information available when they need it, but not when they don't need it, because that becomes very irritating.

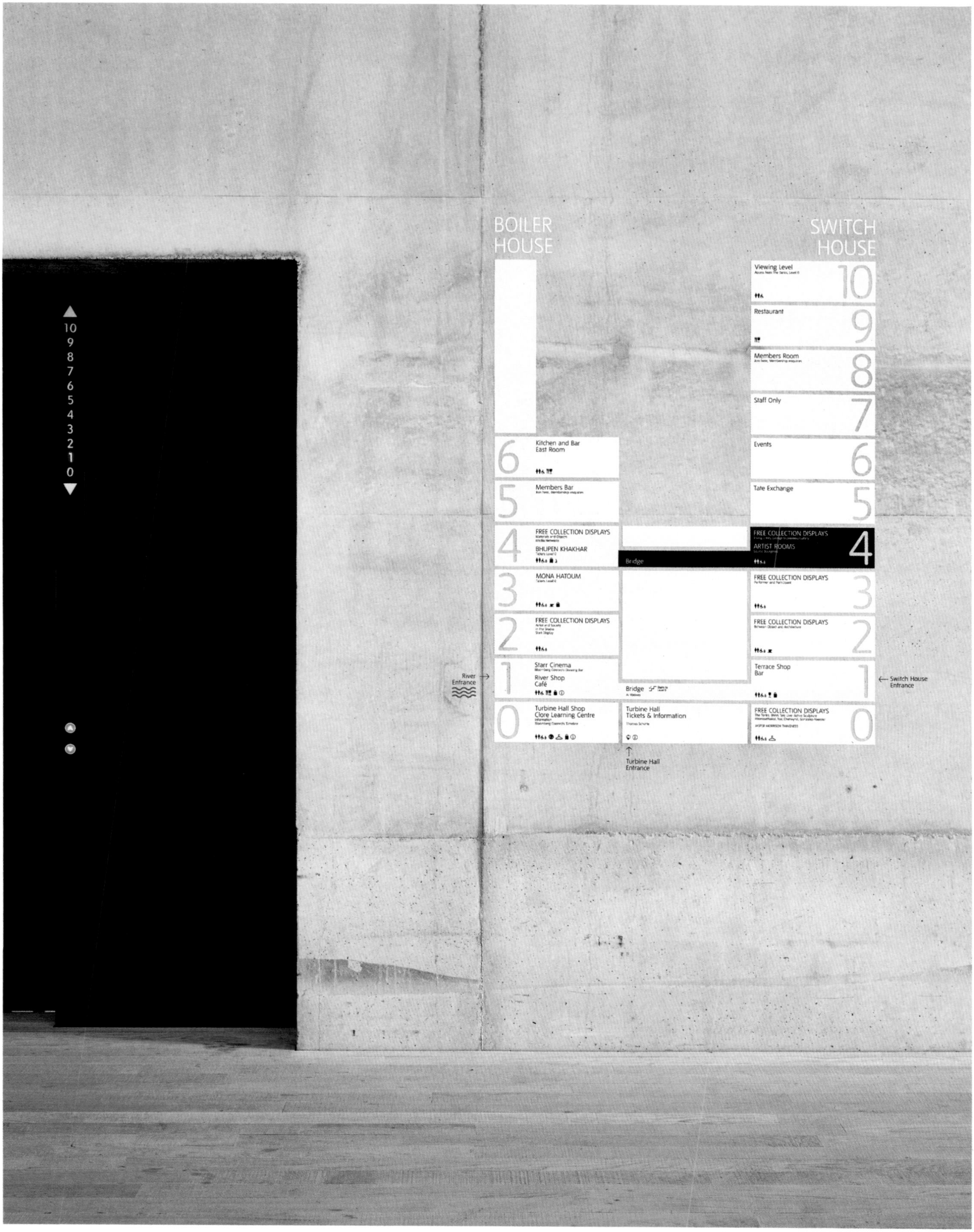

▲

10
9
8
7
6
5
4
3
2
1
0

▼

BOILER HOUSE

SWITCH HOUSE

	Viewing Level — Access from The Tanks, Level 0 — **10**
	Restaurant — **9**
	Members Room — Join here, Membership enquiries — **8**
	Staff Only — **7**
6 — Kitchen and Bar — East Room	Events — **6**
5 — Members Bar — Join here, Membership enquiries	Tate Exchange — **5**
4 — FREE COLLECTION DISPLAYS — BHUPEN KHAKHAR	**FREE COLLECTION DISPLAYS — ARTIST ROOMS — 4**
	Bridge
3 — MONA HATOUM	FREE COLLECTION DISPLAYS — Performer and Participant — **3**
2 — FREE COLLECTION DISPLAYS — Artist and Society — In the Studio — Start Display	FREE COLLECTION DISPLAYS — Between Object and Architecture — **2**
1 — Starr Cinema — River Shop — Café	Terrace Shop — Bar — **1**
	Bridge
0 — Turbine Hall Shop — Clore Learning Centre	Turbine Hall — Tickets & Information	FREE COLLECTION DISPLAYS — **0**

River Entrance →

← Switch House Entrance

↑ Turbine Hall Entrance

I think the museum is a perfect place for the 'slow experience', an experience that can unfold. Exploring is a natural human process and visitors should be allowed to do this in their own time. You want visitors to find their chosen destination easily, but you also want them to go somewhere that they weren't necessarily intending to go; this is about surprise and delight.

Chris Dercon In the past, in most museums of modern and contemporary art there were many art objects shocking and separating visitors. Now museums in general are expressing co-operation. They embrace visitors. And people flock to museums, not to shut off from their life, but to feel closer to it. That means an ever-growing responsibility for Tate, especially in a city like London, where the public realm is almost completely disappearing.

Ian Cartlidge That's true. I think Tate Modern is, and should be, leading the way here. Tate Modern has helped to regenerate a whole urban district in London. It's bigger than its four walls. It reaches right out and it becomes a part of people's lives. You don't necessarily say 'I'm going to Tate Modern today to see a specific artist or show'; you can still do that, but it is now enough to say 'I'm going to Tate Modern today' – where a whole set of experiences and possibilities will unfold.

Chris Dercon Public funding continues to diminish. At the same time the idea of public domain is going down the drain. Is Tate Modern the last museum of its kind? Is Tate Modern the end of an era?

Ian Cartlidge Well, it's a bit depressing to think about it that way. But then how many more Tate Moderns can there possibly be? It's quite unique. It's a unique project!

End.

The Switch House staircase, Level 0.

The Switch House, level 2, with works by (from left to right) Li Yuan-chia, Mary Martin, Marisa Merz, Yayoi Kusama, David Medalla, Amalia Pica.

The Switch House, Level 3.

The Switch House, Level 4.

The Wolfson Gallery in the Switch House, level 3, with work by Ana Lupas.

The George Economou Gallery in the Switch House, level 4, with works by Marwan Rechmaoui (foreground) and Nil Yalter (background).

The Switch House, level 4.

The Switch House, level 4.

The Switch House, level 3.

Looking east from level 10 of the Switch House, over the Turbine Hall roof and the Boiler House Members Bar terrace.

The Switch House, level 10.

The Peter and Maria Kellner Bridge, level 4.

186   The Kitchen and Bar in the Boiler House, level 6.

The Joseph Beuys ARTIST ROOM in the Boiler House, level 2.

The Boiler House, level 2.

Ai Weiwei's *Tree* 2010 on the Turbine Hall Bridge.

1 Tate Modern
2 St Paul's Cathedral
3 River Thames

0 25 50   100

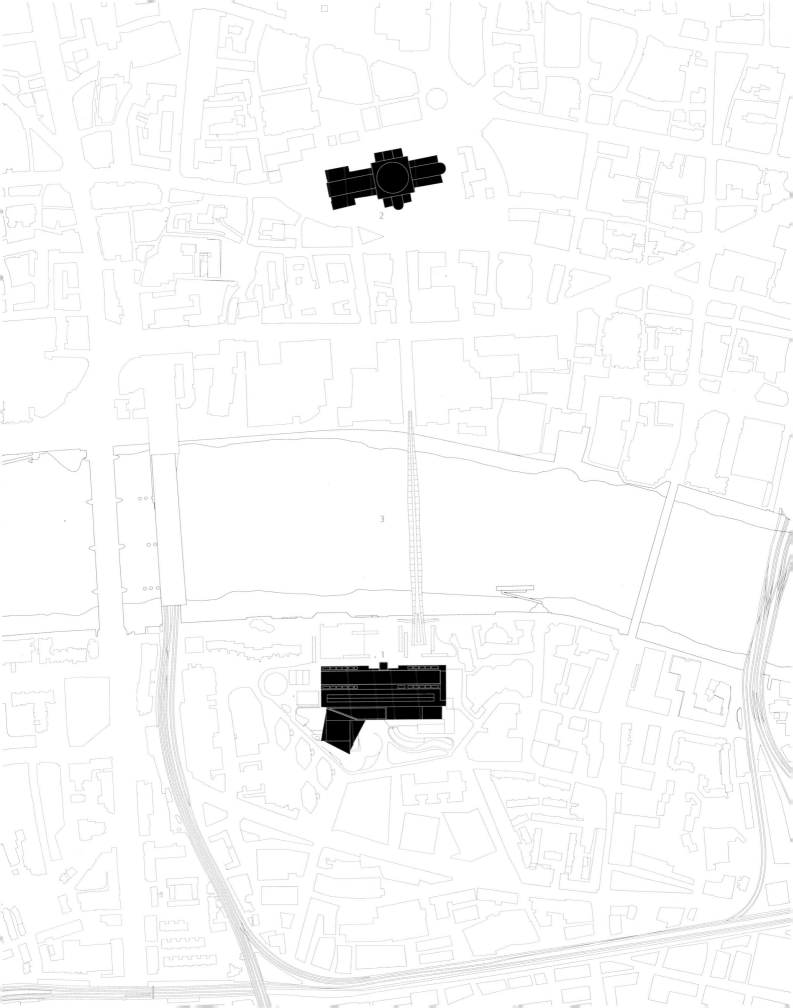

0   25   50   100

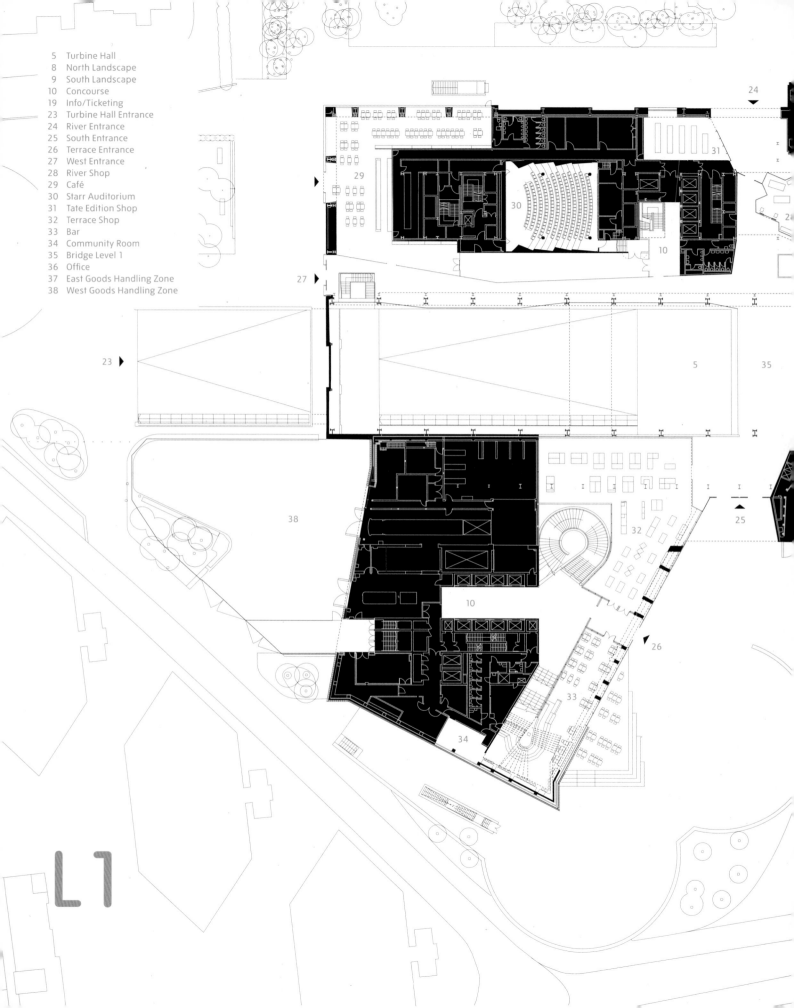

L1

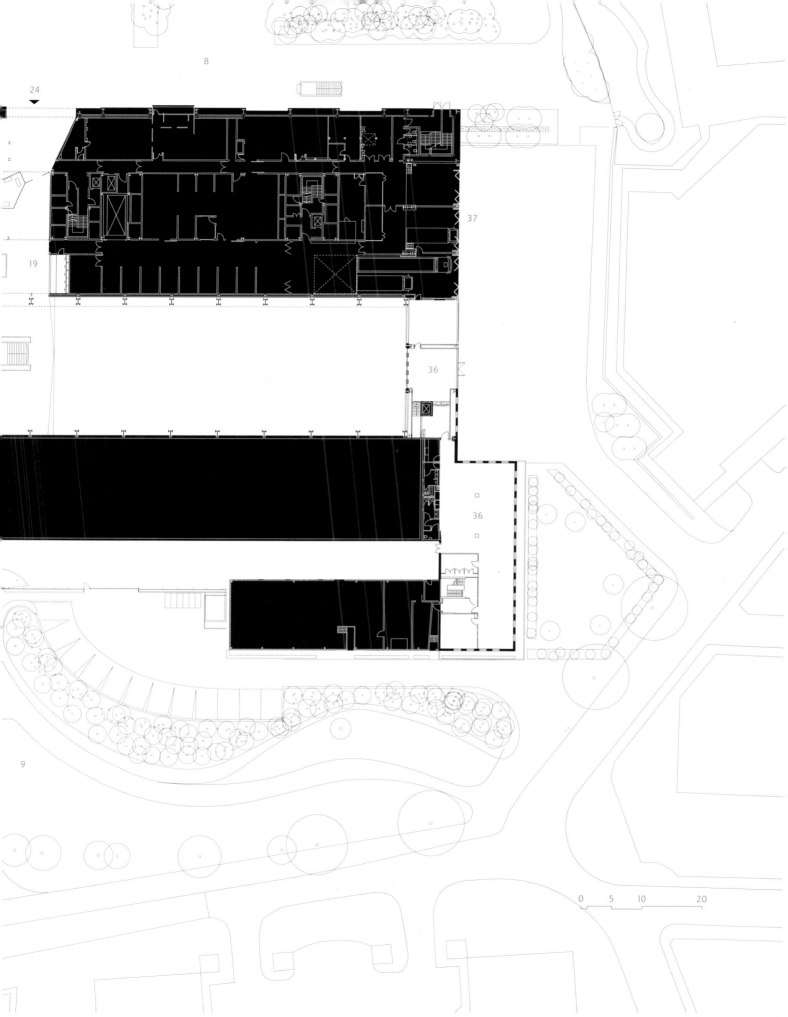

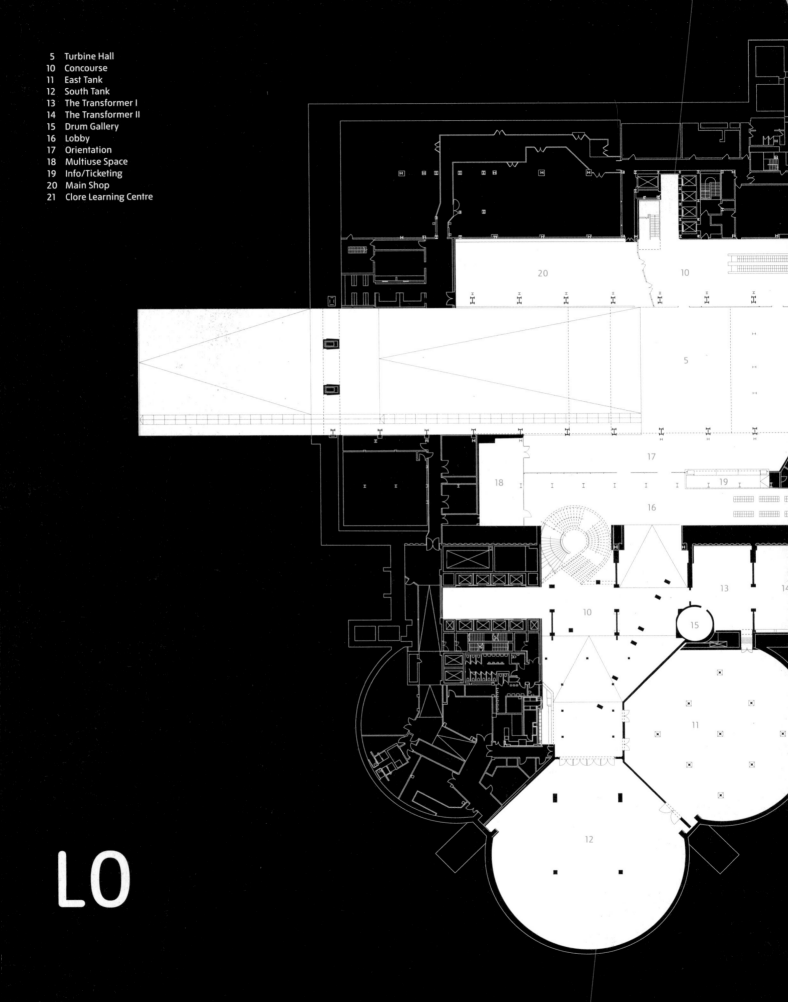

LO

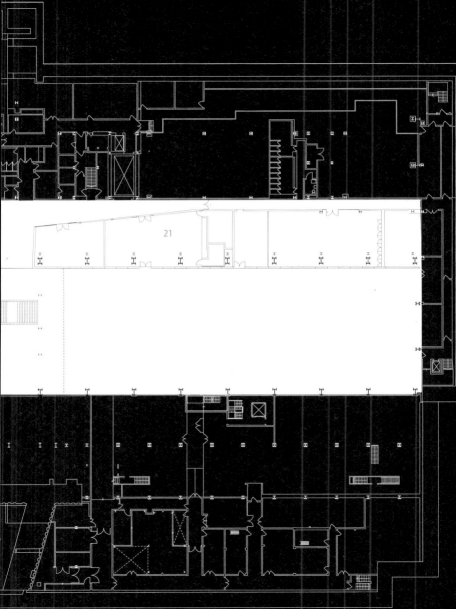

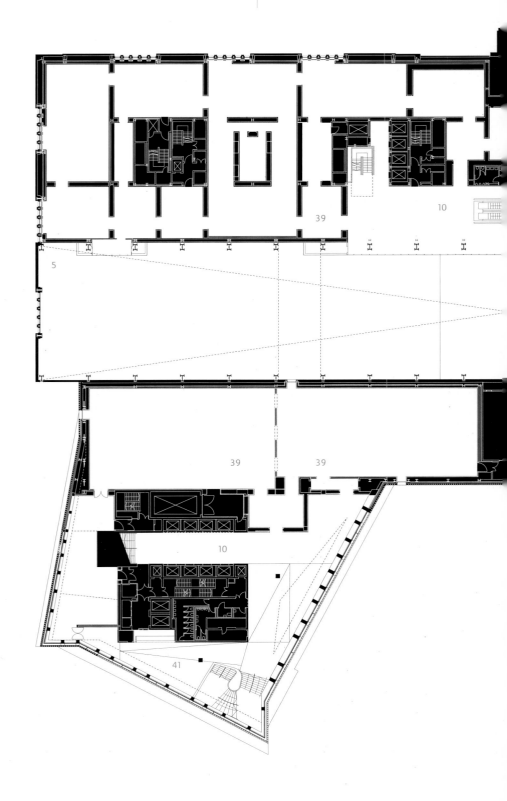

A

5

39

39

10

10

41

L2

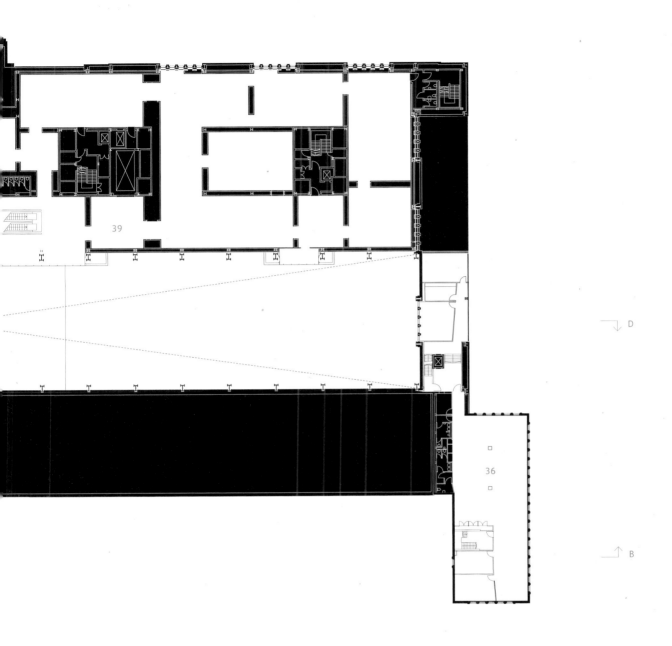

39

36

D

B

0   5   10   20

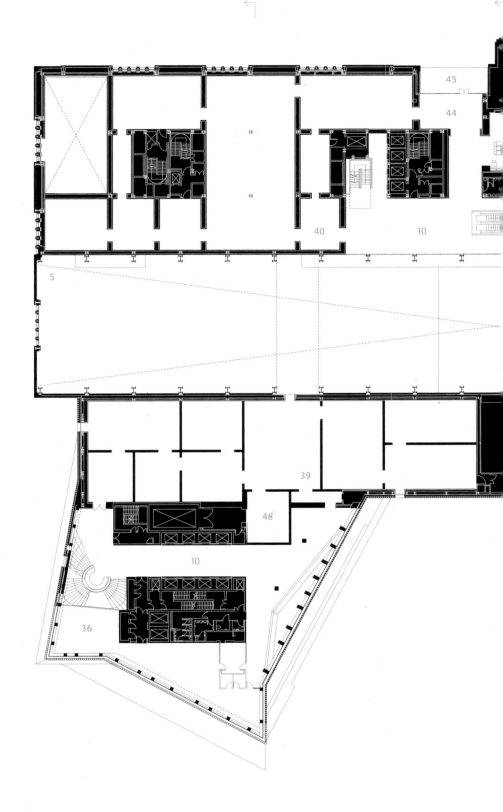

L3

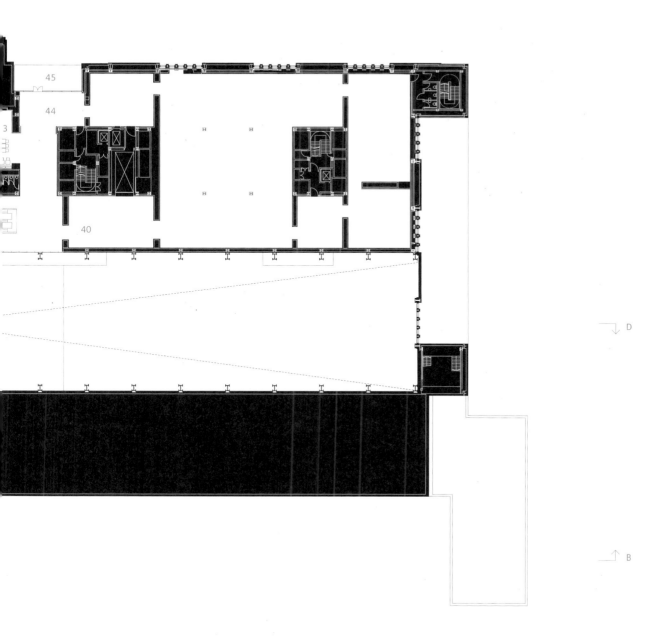

45

44

40

D

B

0   5   10   20

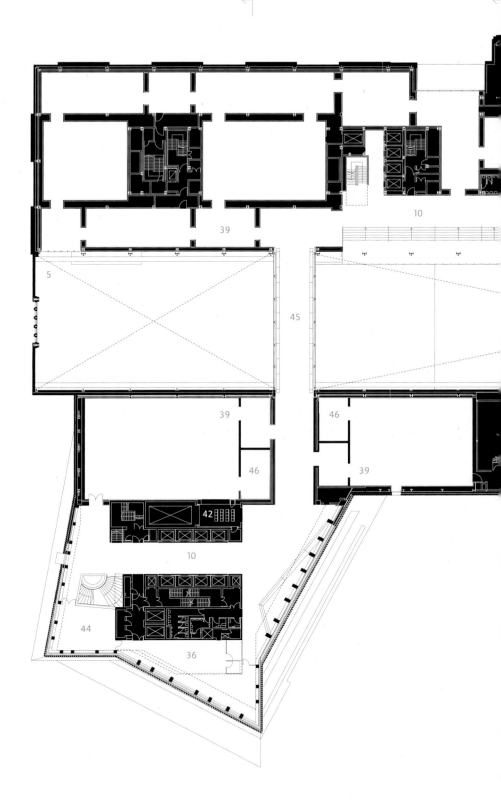

L4

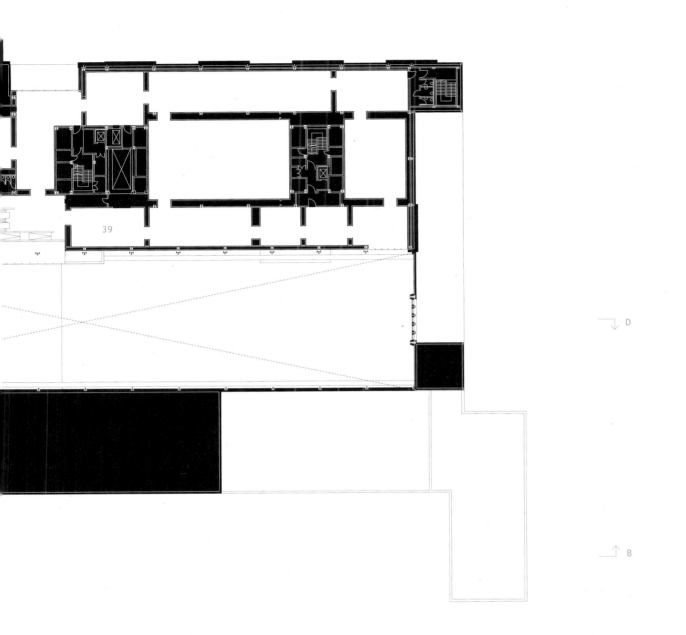

39

D

B

0   5   10   20

A

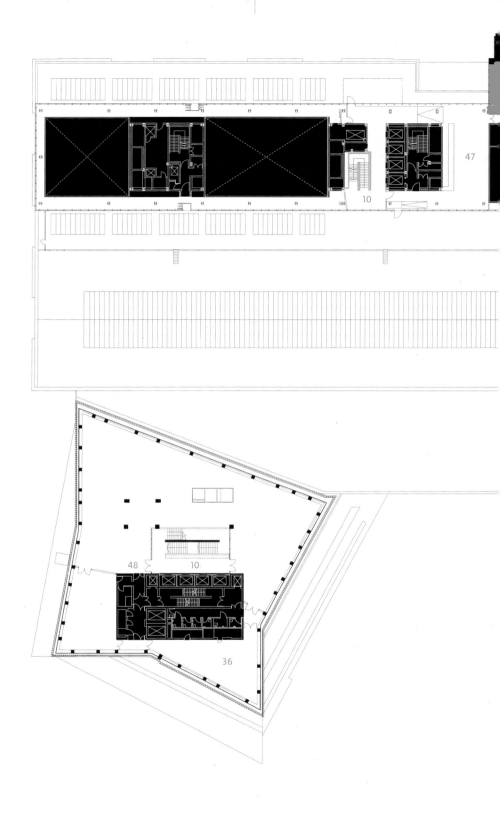

47

10

48   10

36

L5

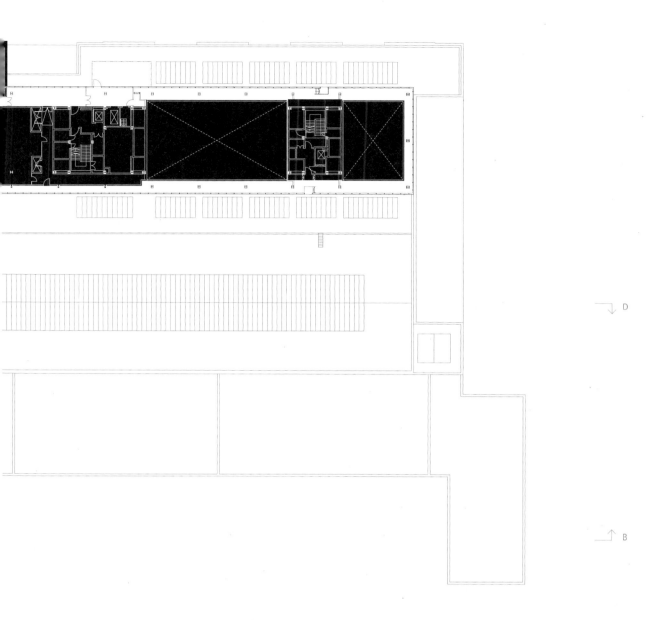

0   5   10   20

A

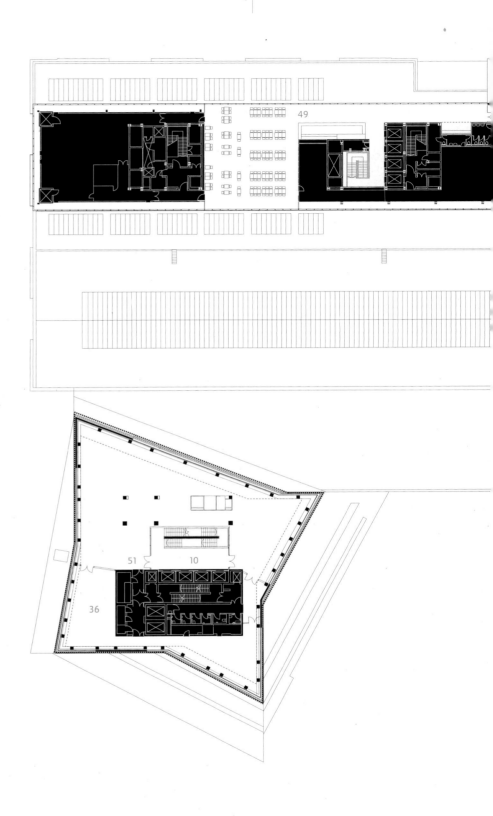

49

51 10

36

L6

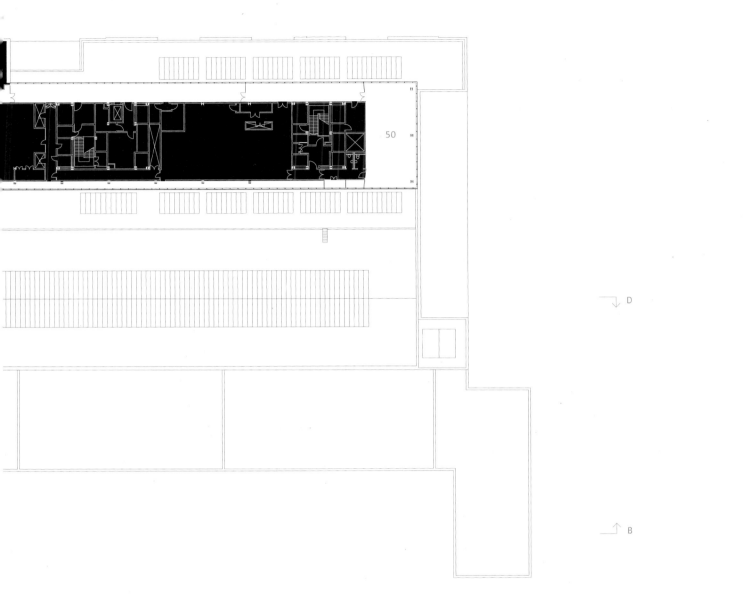

50

↓ D

↑ B

0   5   10   20

10 Concourse
52 Staff Restaurant
53 Storage

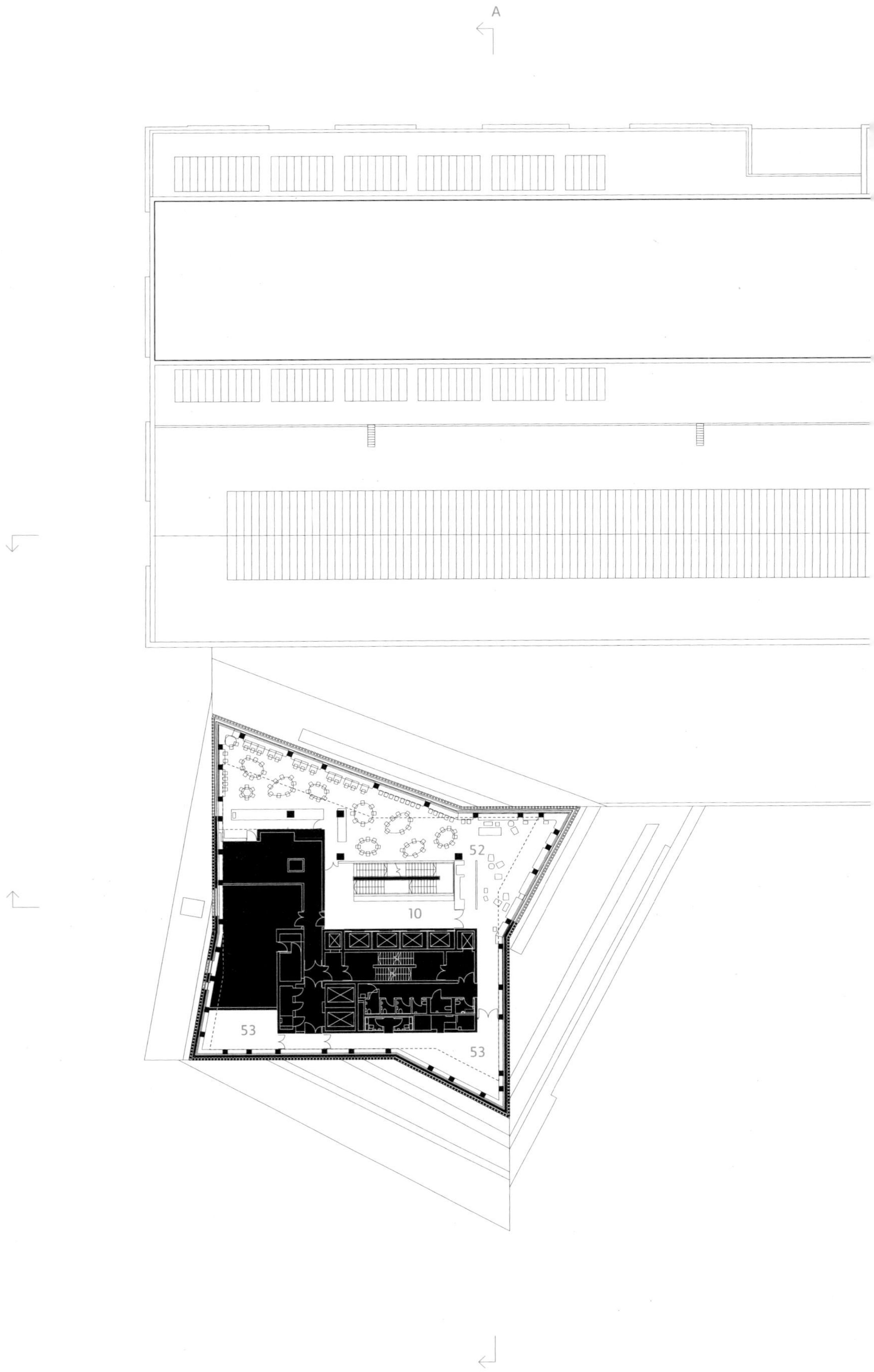

L7

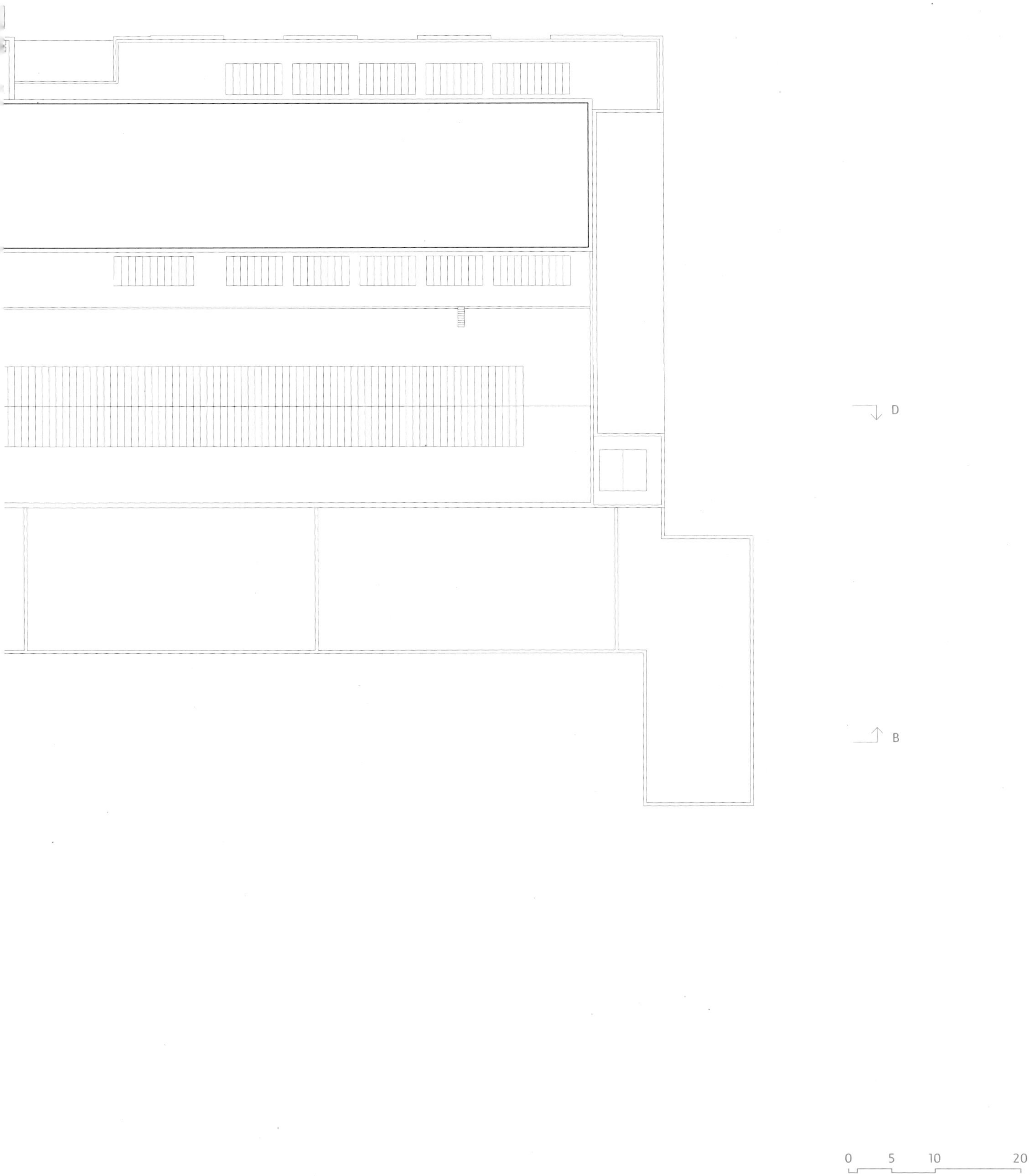

D

B

0   5   10   20

A

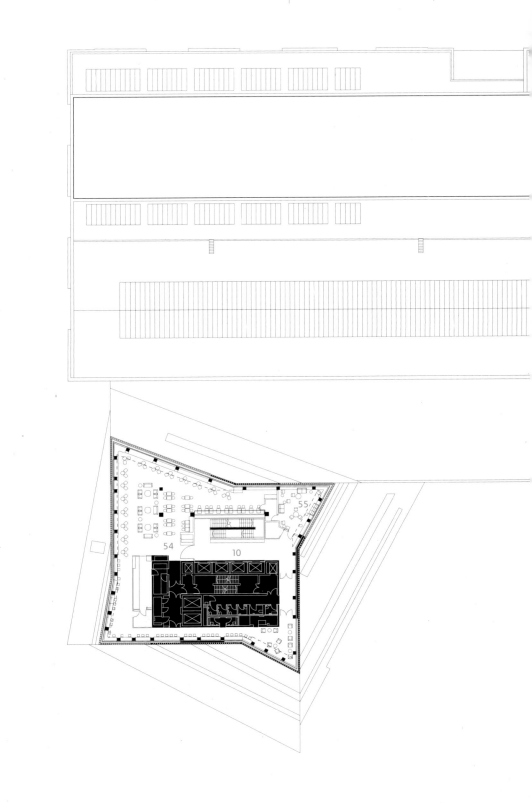

54

10

55

L8

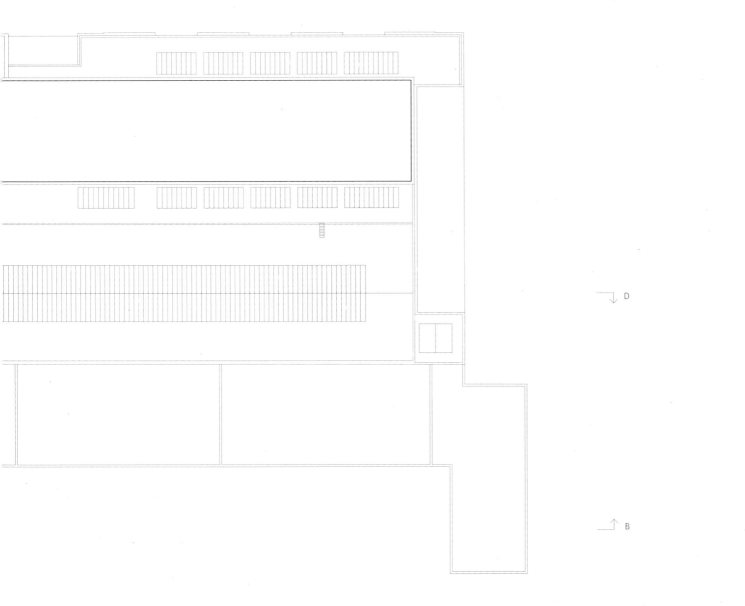

D

B

0   5   10   20

A

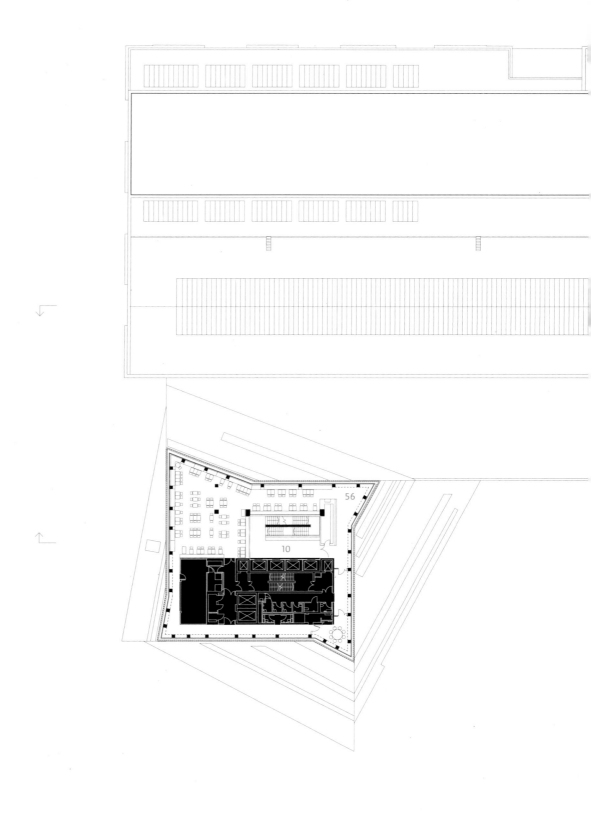

L9

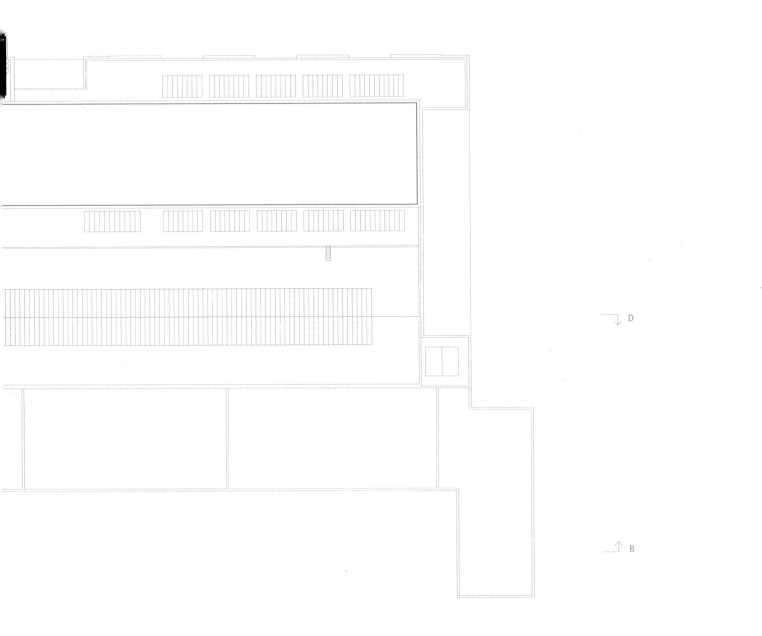

D

B

0   5   10   20

A

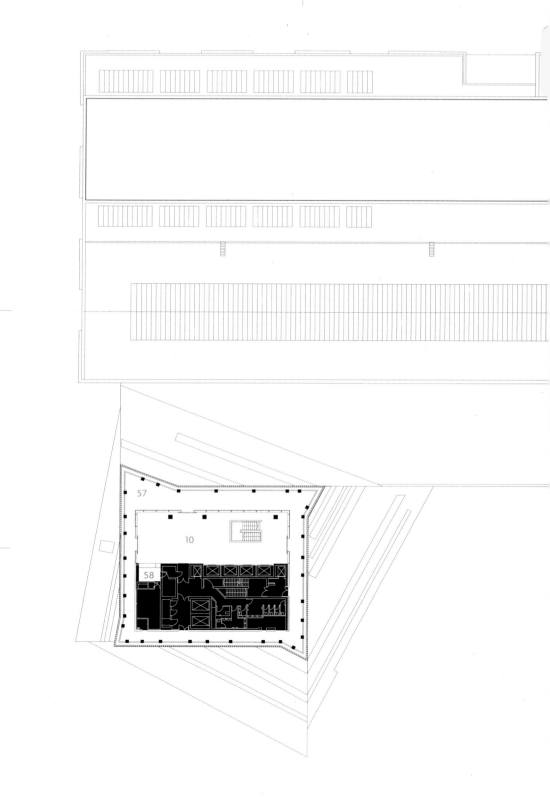

L10

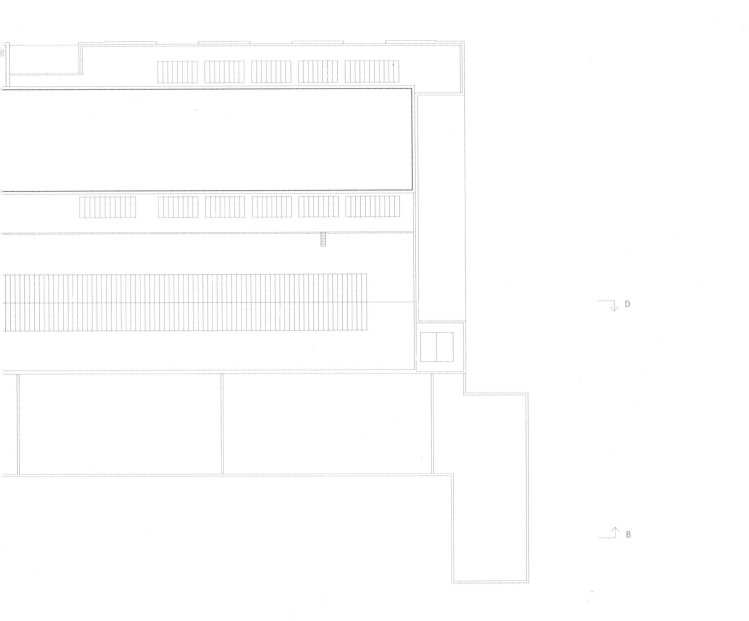

D

B

0   5   10   20

5	Turbine Hall	20	Main Shop	36	Office	52	Staff Restaurant
10	Concourse	22	Entrance to Tanks	39	Collection	53	Storage
11	East Tank	23	Turbine Hall Entrance	40	Exhibition	54	Members Room
12	South Tank	25	Terrace Entrance	45	Bridge Level 4	55	Patrons Room
13	The Transfomrer I	28	River Shop	46	Interpretation Space	56	Restaurant
14	The Transformer II	30	Starr Cinema	47	Members Room	57	Viewing Terrace
16	Lobby	32	Terrace Shop	48	Tate Exchange		
17	Orientation	33	Bar	49	Restaurant		
19	Info and Ticketing	35	Bridge Level 1	51	Tate Studio		

Section A

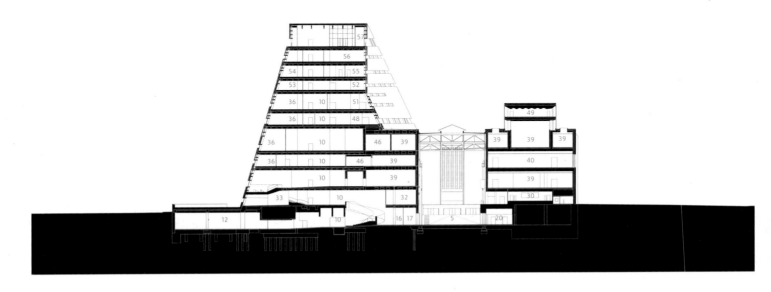

Section B

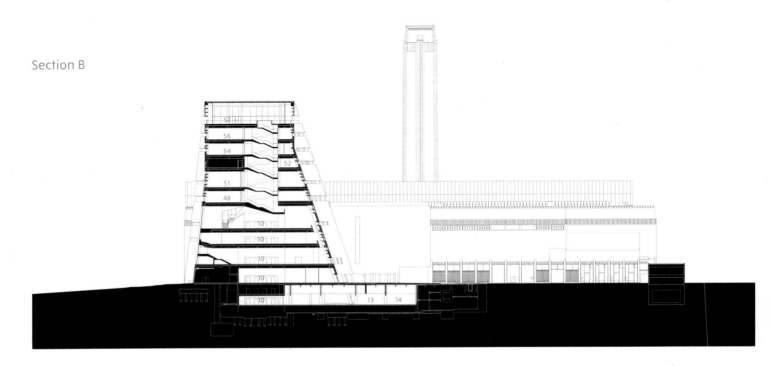

Section C

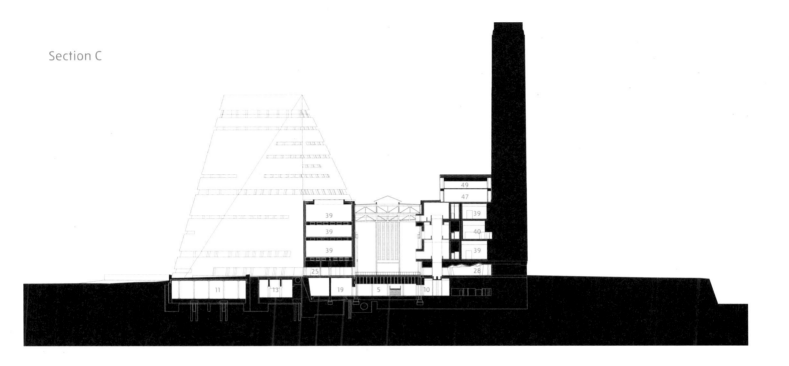

Section D

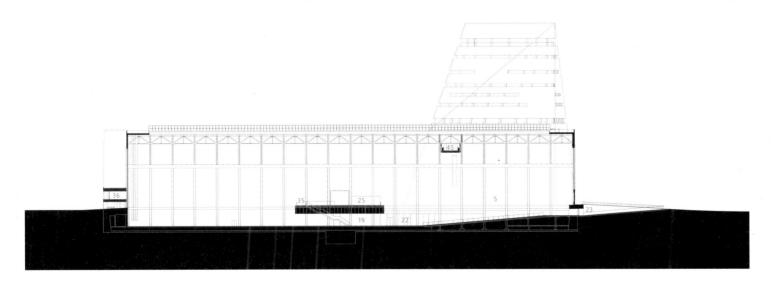

The Boiler House and Turbine Hall Facts and Figures

Tate Modern Design Team

Client
Tate Gallery Projects Ltd
Director: Nicholas Serota
Director of Buildings and
Gallery Services: Peter Wilson
Project Director: Dawn Austwick

Architect
Herzog & de Meuron
Partners: Jacques Herzog,
Pierre de Meuron, Harry Gugger
(Partner in Charge)
Christine Binswanger
Project Team: Michael Casey
(Associate, Project Architect)
Thomas Baldauf, Ed Burton,
Victoria Castro, Emanuel Christ,
Peter Cookson, Irina Davidovici,
Liam Dewar, Catherine Fierens,
Hernan Fierro, Adam Firth,
Matthias Gnehm, Nik Graber,
Konstantin Karagiannis,
Angelika Krestas, Patrik Linggi,
José Ojeda Martos, Mario
Meier, Filipa Mourao, Yvonne
Rudolf, Juan Salgado, Vicky
Thornton, Kristen Whittle,
Camillo Zanardini

Associate Architect
Sheppard Robson
Senior Partner: Richard Young

Interior Design
Herzog & de Meuron in
collaboration with Office for
Design, Jasper Morrison

Engineer
Ove Arup & Partners
Directors: John Hirst,
Tony Marriott

Cost Consultant
Davis, Langdon & Everest
Partners: Ian Fraser,
Paul Morrell

Project Manager
Stanhope plc
Andy Butler, Ron German,
Stuart Lipton, Peter Rogers

Construction Manager
Schal International
Management Ltd
Project Managers: Ian Blake,
Ken Doyle, Mike O'Rorke,
Dale Sager, Nick Woolcott

Landscape Architect
concept design
Herzog & de Meuron with
Kienast Vogt Partner
Partners: Dieter Kienast,
Günther Vogt; detailed design:
Kienast Vogt Partner with
Charles Funke Associates

Fit-Out Manager
Interior plc
Project Manager: Steve Howe

Bankside Power Station

3.48 hectare site on the south
side of the River Thames
opposite St Paul's Cathedral

Northern frontage of site over
200 m long

16,100 m² total floorplate, of
which 3,065 m² given over
to existing London Electricity
sub-station

Height of Turbine Hall from
ground level 26 m

Chimney 99 m high, built to be
lower than St Paul's 114 m

Approximately 4.2 million
bricks

Total area of basements
underneath the turbine hall,
boiler house and sub-station
approximately 1.1 hectares,
with average depth of 8.5 m

3 oil storage tanks with a total
floorplate of approximately
0.36 hectares

3 × 60 MW turbines

1 × 120 MW turbine

4 × 420 Klb/hour oil-fired
boilers

1 × 860 Klb/hour oil-fired boiler

Over 10,000,000 kg of metal
removed, which was either
reprocessed or scrapped

Tate Modern

Project Cost
£134.5 million

Design information
Total internal floor area of
approximately 34,500 m²

Display area 12,402 m²
comprising:

Gallery suites for display and
exhibitions totalling 7,827 m²

Turbine Hall 3,300 m²

Concourse areas on Levels 3,
4 and 5 totalling 1,275 m²

Auditorium to seat 240

Café on Level 6 to seat 170
plus 30 in the bar area

Café on Level 1 to seat 240

Three shops
Level 0, 500 m²; Level 1,
300 m²; Level 3 exhibition shop,
150 m²

Education 390 m²

Members Room 150 m²

Office 1,350 m²

Support services/art handling
935 m²

Floor by Floor

Turbine Hall (Level 0)*
Length 155 m; width 23 m;
height 35 m

2 × gantry cranes originally to
service the turbines, one able
to lift up to 20,300 kg, the other
up to 50,800 kg

Level 0
Shop, reception and cloakroom
facilities, education area,
information, membership,
sound guide, ticketing and
orientation, plant

Level 1
Café, auditorium, shop, film/
seminar room, art management
and loading bay

Level 2
Two display suites for the
Collection, 28 (variable)
galleries with a total area of
2,785.2 m², gallery heights
5.2 m apart from one gallery
of 13 m, concourse of 425 m²

Level 3
Two display suites for
temporary exhibitions,
26 (variable) galleries with a
total area of 2,426.4 m², all
galleries are 4.9 m high,
Espresso Bar, Exhibition Shop,
terraces, concourse of 425 m²

Level 4
Two display suites for the
Collection, 30 (variable)
galleries with a total area of
2,602.5 m², various gallery
heights of 4.7 m, 4.9 m, 9.4 m,
concourse of 425 m²

Level 5
Members Room (with terraces),
plant

Level 6
Café and entertainment
facilities

Structure and Materials

5,000 tons of new steel work

17,000 m³ of concrete poured

Level 5 gallery Silidur conductil steel fibre concrete floor topping 2,800 m² placed and finished in three pours

10,500 m² new timber floor in all areas

Level 2 and 3 galleries and all concourse areas 70 × 12 mm rough-sawn, square-edged, unfinished oak planks

62,400 m² of drylining

21 different types of glass used, varying in thickness between 6 and 45 mm with light transmission values between 8% and 86%

Glazed walls of 8,200 m²

15,000 lights

Total length of cabling approximately 350 km

399 cast iron floor grilles

3,700 fire sprinkler heads

Staircase with 220 stairs

1,500 internal doors

9 passenger lifts of which 4 for public use (capacity of each 16 people), 2 goods lifts (one for art handling, capacity 20 tons.

6 escalators

Turbine Hall roof light consisting of 524 glass panes

Landscape planting
20,000 daffodil bulbs
894 yew hedging plants
1,423 ornamental apple
1,570 ornamental quince
870 dogwood
10 magnolia

1,035 silver birch in bosques
108 specimen silver birch
plus other species including box, hydrangea, honeysuckle, virginia creeper, clematis and various perennials

*The Level numbering changed in 2012, with the opening of the Tanks. Originally starting with the Turbine Hall and Level 1, rising to Level 7, they were relabelled Levels 0–6.

The Switch House and Tanks Facts and Figures

Tate Modern Design Team

Client
Trustees of the Tate Gallery
Director, Tate: Nicholas Serota
Managing Director, Tate:
Alex Beard/Kerstin Mogull
Director of Finance and Estates,
Tate: Stephen Wingfield

Architect
Herzog & de Meuron
Partners: Jacques Herzog,
Pierre de Meuron,
Ascan Mergenthaler
(Partner in Charge)
Harry Gugger (until 2009)
Project Team: John O'Mara
(Associate, Project Director),
Kwamina Monney
(Project Manager),
Ben Duckworth (Associate),
Christoph Zeller

Landscape Architect
Vogt

Furniture Design
Jasper Morrison Studio

Wayfinding and Signage Design
Cartlidge Levene with Morag
Myerscough

Retail Design
Uxus

Structural Engineers
Ramboll UK

Building Services Engineers
Environmental Design
& Sustainability
Max Fordham LLP

Cost Consultant
Aecom

Project Manager
GTMS

Construction Manager
Mace

Client Advisor
Stanhope plc

New Tate Modern/ Switch House and Tanks

Project Budget
£260 million

Design Information
Switch House
Total internal floor area of
approximately 23,600 m²

Boiler House and Turbine Hall
Total internal floor area of
approximately 34,500 m²

Display area in the Switch
House comprising:
Tanks at Level 0: 1,805 m²
Galleries on Levels 2, 3 and 4:
3,500 m²

Introductory room
on Level 2 103 m²

Interpretation room
on Level 3 78 m²

Interpretation room
on Level 4 40 m²

Screening Room on Level 4
to seat 20 people 26 m²

Concourse areas that can also
be used for display purposes
4,980 m²

Restaurant on Level 9
to seat 140 394 m²

Bar on Level 1 to seat 70
250 m² with a terrace
to seat 40

Espresso bar on Level 2

Espresso bar on Viewing Level
Crush Bar in the Tanks

Shop on Level 1 495 m²

Exhibition Shop
on Level 2 207 m²

Learning
Level 5 754 m²; Level 6 473 m²

Community Room
Level 1 33 m²

Members Room
Level 8 to seat 150 456 m²

Staff Offices
Levels 3, 4, 5 and 6
totalling 926 m²

Staff Facilities
Level 7 390 m²

Art Handling Areas
443 m²

Floor by Floor

Level 0
The Tanks: South Tank gallery,
East Tank gallery, Transformer
Galleries, Drum Gallery.
Lobby and lockers, Public Stair,
Bar, Photography studio,
dressing rooms, green room
and performance storage

Level 1
Public Terraces and parks,
South Entrance, Terrace
Entrance, Bar, Terrace Shop,
Community Room, Loading
bays and art management
areas

Level 2
One large flexible gallery to
display the Collection or
temporary exhibitions, one
area to display the Collection or
use as a retail space, Concourse,
Void, Espresso Bar

Level 2 mezzanine
Staff lockers

Level 3
Nine flexible galleries to
display the Collection,
Interpretation space,
Concourse, Void, Staff offices

Level 4
Two large galleries to display
the Collection, one of which
will show Artist Rooms, one
interpretation space, one
screening room, concourse
leading to the bridge over the
Turbine Hall, Staff offices

Level 4 mezzanine
Staff offices and lockers

Level 5
Learning area for Tate Exchange,
Staff offices

Level 6
Learning area or space for
events, Staff offices

Level 6 mezzanine
Staff facilities

Level 7
Staff Facilities

Level 8
Members room,
Benefactors room

Level 9
Restaurant

Level 10
Viewing Level, Espresso Bar

Structure and Materials

19,063 m³ of concrete

2,916 tonnes of reinforcement

923 pre-cast concrete beams

225 pre-cast concrete columns

1,109 pre-cast concrete panels

337,000 bricks

168,500 blocks

3,500 m² external glazing

8,496 m² of new timber floor
in all areas; Levels 2, 3 and 4
galleries and all concourses
areas 70 × 12 mm rough-sewn,
square edged, unfinished
oak planks

19,900 m² drylined walls

9,000 lights

130,000 km of cabling

578 iron floor grilles

3,009 sprinkler heads

Public staircase with 439 steps

343 internal doors

40 shutters

8 passenger lifts, 3 goods lifts, one for art handling

95 toilets

Sustainability

5,309,378 kWh usage a year from electricity

1,502,354 tonnes of carbon per year

25% less energy and carbon than current regulations

Energy saving of 40% compared with Tate Modern Boiler House

40% of naturally ventilated space

18% of predicted energy use will be for cooling the building

100% of cooling will be provided from groundwater

14,752 kg of waste produced every week

Rainwater falling on the roof stored for toilet flushing

Thermal mass in building's concrete finishes provide passive cooling

Landscaping

Entire new South and West Landscape 15,000 m²

11,000 m² asphalt and paving

1,515 m² grass

150 m of oil tank wall

72 bike racks

Trees
9 London plane
2 American plane
3 Oriental plane
3 sycamore maple

Hedges
32 field maple
32 European hornbeam
32 Cornelian cherry
32 European beech
32 European privet
32 common hawthorn
80 ivy

Spine Planting, South
23 white-barked Himalayan birch
20 monarch birch
22 paper birch
168 silver birch
23 Chinese red birch

Mixed Ground Flora Planting
120 blue bugle
80 wild garlic
200 lily of the valley
80 common snowdrop
280 hyacinth
120 wild daffodil
160 primula

Lawn
Species Rich Grass
(1,515m² seeded)

Festuca rubra subspecies *commutata*
Festuca rubra subspecies *trichophylla*
Lollium perenne

Furniture

All built-in furniture designed by Herzog & de Meuron. All other furniture designed by Jasper Morrison except where indicated in *italic*; date of original design in brackets; manufacturers' names in magenta

Maruni
38 Botan benches (2016)
3 Bruno sofas (2015)

Cappellini
20 leather gallery benches (2014)
8 Morrison stools (2003)
75 Tate thin cushions (2016)
38 Tate thick cushions (2016)

Muji
87 wooden dining chairs without arms (2014)
10 wooden dining chairs with arms (2014)
30 wooden lounge chairs (2014)

Vitra
40 Landi chairs *Hans Corey* (2011)
20 Landi tables *Michel Charlot* (2011)
90 HAL ply chairs (2011)
66 HAL ply stools (2011)
8 HAL armchairs (2014)
55 rectangular Bistro tables *Bouroullec brothers* (2014)
79 Superfold tables (2014)
10 occasional tables (2015)

Nikari
9 December chairs (2013)

Fredericia
9 Pon tables (2015)

PP Mobiler
23 tray tables *Hans J. Wegner*

Bespoke
Private dining table (2016)

Fritz Hansen
3 low tables *Piet Hein and Bruno Mathsson*

B&B italia
Bankside sofa and 22 armchairs (2016)

Moorman
Hut coatstand
Konstantin Grcic

Magis
2 Pipe stools (2008)

Aerial view of the partially built power station, 1951, showing the oil tanks on the right.

Chronology

1947

Sir Giles Gilbert Scott's architectural plans for an oil-fired power station are unveiled.

1948

Building begins.

1953

First phase, including the chimney and the western half of the building complete; begins power generation.

1959

Construction of the remaining half of the power station begins.

1962

7 March
Official opening of Bankside Power Station by Her Majesty Queen Elizabeth II.

1981

31 October
Closure due to increased price of oil, making other methods of generating electricity more economical. An electrical substation run by EDF Energy remains on the site in the southern half of the building.

1992

15 December
Tate holds press conference to announce plans to redefine the display of the collection, leading to the creation of a new Tate Gallery of British Art and a new Tate Gallery of Modern Art by the millennium.

1993

The search for suitable premises begins. Various locations are considered, including the area on the south side of Vauxhall Bridge, the Hungerford Bridge car park site on the South Bank, and sites in Docklands and near King's Cross and Euston stations.

February
Department of National Heritage declares that the power station does not merit listing, in spite of representations by English Heritage.

Spring
Making of the BBC television film about the threat to Bankside Power Station, *One Foot in the Past*, in which Francis Carnwath, Deputy Director of the Tate Gallery, is interviewed. He reports on his visit to the power station to Nicholas Serota, who decides to investigate and adds it to the list of possible sites.

July
Trustees of the Tate Gallery visit Bankside Power Station.

1994

28 April
Announcement that Bankside is to be the site for the new Tate Gallery of Modern Art. London Borough of Southwark offers £1.5 million towards development costs.

Bankside Power Station Turbine Hall, 1994, before the turbines were removed.

13 July
International competition to select an architect is launched.

26 September
International jury, chaired by Sir Simon Hornby, chooses thirteen architects from an initial 148 applicants to go forward to the next stage of the competition.

21 November
Six architects chosen as competition finalists:
Tadao Ando (Japan)
David Chipperfield (UK)
Herzog & de Meuron (Switzerland)
Rafael Moneo (Spain)
Office for Metropolitan Architecture – Rem Koolhaas (The Netherlands)
Renzo Piano (Italy).

1995

24 January
Herzog & de Meuron announced as winning architects.

February
Planning permission granted by the London Borough of Southwark for change of use of the power station to an art gallery.

21 February
Selecting an Architect exhibition opens at the Tate Gallery, Millbank.

15 June
Tate Gallery of Modern Art joins a long list of schemes being considered for funding by the Millennium Commission, many of which are far more developed at this stage.

The architects who took part in the first stage of the 1994 competition, with Nicholas Serota in the Turbine Hall.

1 Hiromitsu Kuwata 2 Masataka Yano 3 Julian Harrap 4 Amanda Levete 5 Jan Kaplicky 6 Ricky Burdett
7 Nicholas Grimshaw 8 Shunji Ishida 9 Rick Mather 10 Nicholas Serota 11 John Pringle 12 Michael Craig-Martin
13 Mark Whitby 14 Renzo Piano 15 Jacques Herzog 16 Will Alsop 17 Rem Koolhaas 18 Claudio Silvestrin
19 Rolfe Judd 20 David Chipperfield
Rafael Moneo and Arata Isozaki's teams were also present but cannot be identified.

June
Work begins to remove the power station machinery.

17 July
'Assessing the Economic Impact' report published, indicating that £30–90 million direct economic benefit could result from the development of the Tate Gallery of Modern Art and up to 2,400 jobs be created

English Heritage grant allows temporary repair of roof to prevent further deterioration of the power station.

28 July
Sheppard Robson appointed as Associate Architects.

30 October
£50 million awarded by the Millennium Commission, using funds from the National Lottery to create one of the Commission's 'Landmark' projects. The total project cost at 2000 prices fixed at £130 million, with an opening date of May 2000.

1996

13 March
Herzog & de Meuron unveil detailed plans that are submitted for planning consent.

2 May
Regeneration agency English Partnerships grant £12 million to acquire the site and cover the costs of removal of the machinery.

Planning approval given by Southwark Council.

June
Brick manufacturers approached to create a match for the existing types of brick.

Floor grilles outline detail issued to selected foundries.

July
Announcement that £85 million has been raised towards development costs.

17 July
Inside Bankside, an exhibition of new art inspired by Bankside

Excavation of the Turbine Hall, 1996.

Power Station, opened at the South London Gallery, including works by Dennis Creffield, Anthony Eyton, Deanna Petherbridge, Thomas Struth, Terry Smith and Catherine Yass.

August
Mock-up of rooftop glass structure, the 'light beam', under construction.

31 August
Removal of machinery from the power station complete. Site handed over by Magnox Electric plc to Schal, Tate Gallery of Modern Art construction managers.

2 September
Public open days held – the last chance to see the interior before construction begins.

10 December
Laser projection onto the facade of the power station

and the announcement of the winning design for a new pedestrian bridge. Foster and Partners, Ove Arup & Partners and Sir Anthony Caro selected.

16 December
Herzog & de Meuron open an on-site office.

December
Demolition of outbuildings along north elevation complete.

1997

January
Demolition of Boiler House roof.

February
Demolition of area each side of the chimney, which then stood isolated on its own foundations.

3 February
Industrial Relations and Safety Code of Practice agreement signed.

Tate Gallery of Modern Art
Herzog & de Meuron, January 1995

The front page of Herzog & de Meuron's submission for the second stage of the architectural competition, 1995.

The chimney from inside the Boiler House after demolition of the surrounding fabric, February 1997.

6 February
Over £100 million raised towards funding target.

April
Timber floor samples laid and undergoing foot traffic tests in staff area at Millbank.

June
Discovery of asbestos and poor condition of existing Turbine Hall roof.

3 June
Kienast Vogt Partner appointed to work with Herzog & de Meuron as landscape architects.

August
Asbestos removed allowing works to restart.

Blasting and treatment of existing steelwork complete.

September
Turbine Hall roof demolished and substructure raft begun as foundation.

7 October
Construction officially begins. A time capsule containing plans, photographs and videos relating to the project along with drawings by local schoolchildren and a piece of Swiss mountain crystal provided by the architects is buried in the foundations by Chris Smith, Secretary of State for Culture, Media and Sport.

13 November
Millennium Commission awards bridge scheme £7.1 million grant.

December
Structural steelwork begins to form the new seven floors in the former Boiler House.

1998

January
Decking and floor construction starts.

April
Removal of original boiler house roof trusses completed, allowing the new floors to support fully the existing brick facade.

May
Steelwork for new two-storey glass roof structure begins, as well as glazing of the new Turbine Hall roof.

Lars Nittve appointed Director of Tate Modern.

June
Drylining to level 3 galleries begins.

August
Secondary steelwork for lift installation starts.

September
Levels 6 and 7 air handling plant installation complete.

Cable pulling begins.

Escalator installation begins.

16 September
'Topping out' achieved. Ceremony performed by Nick Raynsford, Minister for London and Construction.

28 September
Art arrives with the first of a series of temporary art projects. Artists' films projected onto the facade of the building.

November
Escalators located in position.

1999

February
Jasper Morrison appointed as furniture consultant.

4 February
The Arts Council of England Lottery Fund awards a £6.2 million grant allowing additional display space on level 3 to be built in time for the opening, raising the total project cost to £134.2 million (increased by the Trustees to £134.5 million in March 2000 in order to cover costs of further enhancements to the building).

March
Auditorium fit-out begins.

May
Turbine Hall bridge stair installed.

Level 3 west galleries completed and environmental control switched on.

Timber floor installation is started.

13 May
Louise Bourgeois announced as the first artist to be commissioned to create a work for the Turbine Hall.

August
Permanent lighting on in most areas of the building.

31 August
Base build works completed.

Fit-out begins.

6 September
Tate staff move into permanent offices.

October
New gallery names announced: Tate Modern and Tate Britain.

23 December
Many areas of the building complete.

2000

January
Site officially handed over to the Tate Gallery by construction managers, Schal.

Installation of art begins.

11 May
Tate Modern is opened by Her Majesty Queen Elizabeth II.

Laser display for the opening of Tate Modern on 11 May 2000.

10 June
Millennium Bridge opened, designed by Foster + Partners, but closed on 12 June for remedial work because of unexpected swaying caused by the synchronised movement of large numbers of pedestrians.

2002

22 February
Millennium Bridge reopened.

2003

April
Vicente Todolí becomes Director of Tate Modern.

2004

July
Trustees agree objectives and fundraising targets for 'Transforming Tate Modern', the development of the oil tanks and a new extension to Tate Modern.

2006

February
Work on the main brief starts.

Around 2,000 people trying to make the Millennium Bridge wobble as engineers tested the reinforced structure on 30 January 2002.

August
Draft Procurement Strategy produced by Davis Langdon.

October
Gardiner & Theobald appointed as Construction Project Managers.

Brief completed.

2007

April
Business Case for 'Transforming Tate Modern' submitted to the Department of Culture, Media and Sport (DCMS).

July
Expressions of Interest for the Design Team placed in the Official Journal of the European Union (OJEU). Four practices shortlisted: Richard Rogers Partnership; Herzog & de Meuron; Dominique Perrault; and Wilkinson Eyre.

August
The Business Case for 'Transforming Tate Modern' is approved by DCMS and the Treasury as part of the approval process for the capital project.

Jeremy Deller's Acid Brass playing at one of the opening events in May 2000. Louise Bourgeois's sculpture *I do, I Redo, I Undo* 1999–2000 was the first of The Unilever Series of commissions for the Turbine Hall.

Planning Consent for original glass scheme granted.

2008

January
Herzog & de Meuron appointed as architects for the detailed design and construction phase of the scheme.

July
RIBA Design Stage C for present design completed.

UK Government announces grant of £50 million towards the costs of the project.

2009

January
RIBA Design Stage D completed.

Planning application for present scheme submitted to London Borough of Southwark.

May
Planning consent for present scheme granted by London Borough of Southwark.

September
RIBA Stage E completed.

December
Construction work on the Tate Modern Project begins inside the existing Tate Modern building with the works required to strengthen the southern wall of the Turbine Hall is in preparation for the extension. Tate Modern remains open to the public.

The beginning of construction is celebrated by the Mayor of London, Boris Johnson, breaking ground on the South Lawn.

The opening up and demolition of the oil tank lids begins.

Opening up and demolition of the oil tank lids, 2010.

2010

January
Full construction site is established. The main works site is established with the Turbine Hall strengthening works and demolition work of the oil tank lids continuing.

Live site photography is in place and the artist Martin Karlsson's project is installed on the site hoardings.

£76 million of funding has been raised.

February
Enabling works begin.

March
The Trustees confirm that the project should proceed and agree to a first phase of works to complete the Tanks within a budget of £80 million. A decision on the second phase of the project will be made in March 2011.

Plans for an inaugural Tanks artistic programme begin.

Jasper Morrison is appointed as furniture designer.

May
Tate Modern celebrates ten years.

A display of the Tate Modern Project designed by Ab Rogers is launched at Tate Modern during the weekend of celebrations.

June–July
Major works on site begin with the formation of the foundations for the oil tanks and the new structure which will rise above. A revised overall programme reflecting the phasing of the project shows a completion date of the Tanks for May 2012.

The construction of a full-scale mock-up of the facade begins at Tate Stores.

The site is opened to the public to view during London Festival of Architecture week.

Uxus are appointed as retail consultants to work with Herzog & de Meuron on the shops within the new building.

August
The demolition work is complete, the foundation

The abandoned electricity switch house, c.2010.

works are progressing well and further below ground sub-structure works commence.

Cartlidge Levene with Studio Myerscough are appointed as Wayfinding Consultants.

Sevil Peach works with Herzog & de Meuron on the design of the offices.

The project undergoes a successful review from the Office of Government Commerce with the Delivery Confidence Assessment graded Amber.

September–October
The Turbine Hall wall strengthening works are completed and the site is open to view for the public during Open House London weekend.

November
The Board of Trustees agree to proceed with a revised £90 million budget to achieve the first phase of the project and the opening of the Tanks in May 2012, subject to UK

Power Networks handing over the Switch House building in February 2011.

The initial foundation works are complete and the sub-structure works continue, enabling the oil tank spaces and new 'as found' galleries to form the basement level of the Tate Modern extension.

The full site accommodation is placed on the South Lawn in preparation for the next stage of the project which will include the demolition of the western side of the Switch House, the continuation of the sub-structure works and the repair of the oil tanks.

The initial works of the Tate Modern Project within the existing Tate Modern start. This involves a re-design and fit-out of the existing Tate Modern level 1 Learning Centre and the East Annex offices.

Opening up the oil tanks, 2010.

The control room for the electricity switch house, c.2010.

Aerial view of Tate Modern, September 2011.

December

The design of the project as a whole is complete.

Clore Learning Centre works commence in the existing building.

2011

January

£100 million has been raised.

The piling work in the ground beneath the oil tanks is complete and the sub-structure work has started. This includes the capping of the piles with concrete and creating the huge service trench which will be situated below the floor of the oil tanks.

Following the handover of the south-eastern lawn area back to Tate from UKPN (formerly EDFE), new larger site accommodation is established.

The initial wayfinding and signage concepts have been agreed and the fit-out design is being developed.

February

UKPN hands over the western Switch House. A local press event marking this key milestone in the project is held on 25 February. Demolition of the Switch House can now start.

The capping of the piles is complete and the construction of the core walls within the tanks has started. The salvaged steel columns are being prepared for re-installation in the east oil tank.

Tate and Herzog & de Meuron sign off repair works for the inside of the Tanks performance space, galleries and lobby areas.

March

On 16 March the Trustees agree the basis on which the second phase of the project should proceed, allowing more time for the required funding to be in place but with the objective to retain the completion date of May 2012 for the Tanks.

The demolition of the western end of the Switch House has begun and the site is being prepared for the re-instatement of the Tanks lids.

April

Chris Dercon, the new Director of Tate Modern is in post.

Design work continues on the fit-out, signage and planning and implementation of the artistic programme for the opening of the Tanks in 2012.

May

The Clore Learning Centre is complete; the official opening takes place on 25 May.

September

The Trustees approve the implementation of the second phase of the project, subject to the approval by DCMS of financing.

£160 million raised to date.

The main structures for the Tanks and Transformer galleries are complete. Work continues on the core of the building and steelwork has started on the existing and new buildings. The new services are currently being installed within the service tunnel beneath the Tanks.

Anne Teresa De Keersmaeker, *Fase: Four Movements to the Music of Steve Reich* 1982, performed in the Tanks for 'Art in Action', 2012.

2012

January

The main activity on site is the near completion of the sub-structure works, and pre-construction activity on the superstructure has begun.

Preparations are progressing for installing cranes on the site. Finishes and Builders works within the Tanks areas are progressing.

Tate operations and curatorial teams work with the construction managers on the planning, logistics and installation of the artistic programme for the Tanks, which will open to the public in July.

Construction activity starts on the tower superstructure.

March–April

Press announcement of the artistic programme for the opening of the Tanks.

The launch of the fifteen-week festival of 'Art in Action' will be part of the London 2012 Festival, the culmination of the Cultural Olympiad.

May

Completion of the Tanks.

July

Opening of the Tanks to the public on 17 July.

The superstructure work continues on site above the Tanks. The North Core is complete to level 4 and the South Core to level 3.

83% of the works have been procured.

December

Construction works on the pre-cast concrete perimeter structure above ground continue and the North and South core external walls are complete.

The steelwork to the Switch House reconstruction, which will house the new galleries, has now reached level 5 and the installation of the mechanical and electrical plant has begun within these spaces.

The next major visible part of the construction will be the erection of the concrete components which make up the thirty-five perimeter sloping columns. External walls of both cores of the new building complete.

A 'Lessons Learnt' from the opening and operation of the Tanks has been commissioned. From the end of January until May 2013, the Tanks will remain open to the public for a number of special events.

2013

March
Regular meetings take place with DCMS on the revenue costs of the new building, to prepare for negotiations which will form part of the next Comprehensive Spending Review.

Preparations are underway for the closure of the Turbine Hall and western entrance within the existing Tate Modern to create the new level 4 bridge across the Turbine Hall connecting the existing building with the new extension.

May
Construction activity remains focused on the superstructure above ground. Level 3 slab is complete as are the columns and beams up to Level 2 and the installation of the level 3 atrium balustrade is complete.

Work on the Switch House area is progressing well and the steelwork is very nearly complete.

July
Work on the communications and fundraising campaign to engage the public with the project is in the final stages for launch over the summer.

Construction works are progressing on the perimeter structure of the new building. All perimeter concrete columns are in place up to level 4 of the tower. Crease columns are being installed on the eastern side of the tower, showing the complex geometry of the building. The void space that links the level 2, Level 3 and level 4 concourse is now visible. The concrete balustrade to the void on level 3 is in place and the concrete floor slab on level 3 has been poured.

82% of the facade bricks have been manufactured. The project is 87% procured.

Safety on site remains a very high priority with activity continuing to increase over the coming months. A celebration is held in April to mark 250,000 man hours on site without a RIDDOR (Reporting of Injuries, Diseases and Dangerous Occurrences) accident – a major milestone for the site team.

Steelwork to the Switch House is complete.

2014

January
The complex pre-cast concrete perimeter structure continues to rise up to 8 levels with the panels being placed on the lower levels.

The new bridge on level 4 spanning the Turbine Hall has been completed and the Turbine Hall is re-opened to the public.

February
The grand public staircase which is being poured on site is progressing up the building from levels 1–4.

Detailed planning of the artistic and learning programme is being led by the curatorial team.

Plans for the rehang of all the displays in the existing building are underway, which will include a refurbishment of all the display suites in readiness for the opening of the new building.

A communication strategy has been developed for the launch of the New Tate Modern.

March
The perimeter structure has now reached level 9 and work has started on the final Level 10 at the top of the Switch House. The pre-cast concrete panels continue to be installed, creating the envelope.

Art lift installed and in use.

April
The glazing manufacture is 87% complete.

£202 million has been raised.

94% of the construction works have been procured.

May
The roof-top glazing for the level 4 Gallery West is complete.

Perimeter structure is complete.

July
£203 million has been raised.

August
The grand public staircase leading from levels 0–4 is complete.

September
Target dates have been set to complete the project.

A robust Tate Modern Business Plan and Grant in Aid business case submitted to DCMS and HM Treasury.

16 September
Topping-out ceremony to celebrate the completion of the perimeter structure.

The Switch House at sunrise, with the Shard in the distance, December 2015.

October

A target opening date of June 2016 for the New Tate Modern has been set.

Work on the brickwork installation has started.

Planning for commissioning and handover to Tate begins.

A curatorial-led review of the public spaces in and around the new building takes place with Tate senior management and the wider design teams.

The furniture for the public areas has now been presented to Tate non-executive committees for their comments.

December

The external envelope made up of pre-cast concrete panels is complete.

A letter from the Chancellor of the Exchequer committing government to provide for the running costs of the new building has been received by the Director. The Government will do this with new funds for the arts, that is without prejudice to funding for other arts organisations and museums. The precise sum remains to be negotiated, but the binding commitment is the crucial step that is required to enable Tate to prepare for opening.

2015

January

The concrete perimeter structure, the pre-cast concrete panels and the roof of the Switch House are complete.

The installation of the windows in the facade of the tower is underway.

Works start in the existing Tate Modern to create a new service route connecting the Switch House to the Boiler House.

April

The window installation is complete to level 8 with the exception of level 2 to 4 atrium windows.

The Major Projects Authority conducts a Project Assessment Review resulting in a Delivery Confidence Assessment of Amber.

The list of works from the Tate Collection that will be displayed in the new galleries is finalised.

Initial planning to consider the overall nature of the opening week starts.

May

Work has started on the inside of the building to install the windows overlooking the atrium.

Floor screed is being laid in the new galleries, ready for the timber flooring to be laid.

The perimeter art walls are being built.

June

The external brickwork on the Switch House is nearing completion and the scaffolding on this facade starts to come down.

A new Tate Modern Delivery Board is created to oversee the effective planning of all aspects of client delivery, occupation and running of the new building.

July

The atrium glazing within the Switch House is complete.

A temporary office set up in the Tanks in 2015 for the Tate Modern Project team.

The fit-out is continuing on all the floors.

August

The brickwork installation has reached level 5 on all the elevations and is 53% complete.

The installation of the windows is complete.

The timber floor in the new Level 2 gallery is complete and the coffered ceiling in the level 3 galleries has been finished.

September

Tate Press Conference takes place in the new building announcing the public opening date of the new Tate Modern, 17 June 2016.

A visualisation of the new Tate Modern is created by Peter Saville.

The design for the external wayfinding and the naming of the different parts and entrances of the whole building is agreed.

October

The timber flooring is complete in all the galleries and the stretch fabric ceiling in level 4 galleries is installed.

Permanent floor installation is progressing on all other areas.

Work to pedestrianise Sumner Street on the edge of the new southern landscape starts.

Tate starts the installation of the Information Technology Systems.

Over 300 photovoltaic solar panels are installed on the roof of the Turbine Hall.

November

The new large production kitchen within the existing Tate Modern, which will service the whole of the new building, is complete.

The rehang of the Tate Collection starts in the existing Tate Modern galleries.

Nicholas Serota and Frances Morris placing the last brick at the top of the Switch House, 18 February 2016.

The Major Projects Authority conducts a Performance Assessment Review resulting in a Delivery Confidence Assessment of Amber/Green.

In the Autumn Statement the Chancellor of the Exchequer confirms to Tate that additional funding will be made available to run the new Tate Modern.

Public fundraising campaign launched.

December
Over 500 people are now working on the site.

90% of the brickwork is complete.

The key events during the preview opening week are agreed.

2016

January
The internal glazed screens throughout the Switch House are complete.

The new galleries are complete.

The permanent floors are complete in all areas of the Switch House.

Tate Press Conference takes place in New York and in London.

Artist Rooms Press Conference announces Louise Bourgeois display in the new Tate Modern.

February
The brickwork installation is complete and the over one million pieces of scaffolding start to come down.

Integrated systems testing is complete.

Refreshed Tate visual identity is rolled out.

March
The new building is handed over to Tate Estates.

The installation of the works from the collection starts in the Switch House level 3 galleries.

The fitting out of the new staff offices begins.

April
Frances Morris is appointed Director of Tate Modern.

The new service route and kitchens in the existing Tate Modern are complete.
The fitting out of the new Terrace shop begins.

May
The external works and landscaping are complete.

Practical completion of the whole project.

The public furniture designed by Jasper Morrison arrives from storage and is installed floor by floor.

The signage and wayfinding is installed floor by floor.

Advertising campaign for the opening of the new Tate Modern is launched nationwide.

12–16 June
Friends and Family Day.

Artists Preview.

Press Preview.

Members Preview.

Schools Open Day.

Benefactors Dinner.

Opening Party, broadcast live by the BBC.

17 June
The new Tate Modern opens to the public.

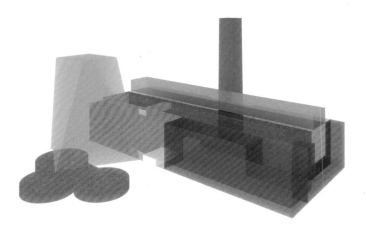

Peter Saville, MULTICOLOUR TM 2016, courtesy of Herzog & de Meuron created with the assistance of Morph and Paul Hetherington.
Peter Saville's three-dimensional interpretation of Tate Modern was commissioned by Tate to mark the opening of the gallery in its new form. The purpose was to convey the message that the larger building is a single entity with new parts that are a natural growth from the original. Saville created a dynamic digital sequence from which a multiplicity of views could be derived.

Schools Open Day, 16 June 2016.

Notes

Oliver Wainwright
Lofts and Caves

1 Ministry of Town and Country Planning, *Bankside generating station: Inspector's report, 1944–47*, http://www.glias.org.uk/gliaspapers/bankside.html, accessed 9 April 2015.

2 'The Bankside Power State. Sir Giles Scott Explains', *The Builder*, 23 May 1947, p.494.

3 Rowan Moore and Raymund Ryan, 'Building Tate Modern', London 2000, p.46.

4 Interview with the author, Basel, 24 August 2015.

5 Jonathan Glancey, *London: Bread and Circuses*, London and New York 2003, p.76.

6 Jonathan Glancey, 'Tate Modern 2, The Epic Sequel', *The Guardian*, 26 July 2006, http://www.theguardian.com/society/2006/jul/26/communities.arts, accessed 10 April 2016.

7 Will Self, 'Are the Hyper-rich Ruining the New Tate Modern?', *The Guardian*, 21 November 2014, http://www.theguardian.com/artanddesign/2014/nov/21/will-self-are-the-hyper-rich-ruining-the-new-tate-modern, accessed 10 April 2016.

8 'Filling the Hole in the Doughnut', *Building Design*, 5 April 2007, http://www.bdonline.co.uk/filling-the-hole-in-the-doughnut/3084323.article, accessed 10 April 2016.

9 Rowan Moore, 'And now ... It's the Tate Hotel', *Evening Standard*, 4 June 2001, http://www.standard.co.uk/showbiz/and-now-its-the-tate-hotel-6348673.html, accessed 10 April 2016.

10 Interview with the author, London, 6 January 2016.

11 Ibid.

12 Interview with the author, London, 1 December 2015.

13 Ibid.

14 Interview with the author, Basel, 24 August 2015.

15 Interview with the author, London, 1 December 2015.

16 Ibid.

17 Interview with the author, Basel, 24 August 2015.

18 Interview with the author, London, 1 December 2015.

19 Interview with the author, Basel, 24 August 2015.

20 Interview with the author, London, 1 December 2015.

21 Objection to the planning application, cited in the Southwark planning officer's report, 27 March 2007; planning ref. 06-AP-1913.

22 Interview with the author, Basel, 24 August 2015.

23 All quotes: interview with the author, Basel, 24 August 2015.

Wouter Davidts
A Ziggurat of Brick and Concrete

1 Marcel Broodthaers, *Lettre Ouverte, Palais des Beaux Arts, Brussels*, 7 June 1968, reproduced in Carel Blotkamp (ed.), *Museum in ¿Motion?: The Modern Art Museum at Issue = museum in ¿beweging?: het museum voor moderne kunst ter diskussie*, 's-Gravenhage Govt. Pub. Office, Netherlands 1979, p.250: 'We play here until the end of the world' (author's translation).

2 Jacques Herzog & Pierre de Meuron, 'Collaborations with Artists, Museum Projects and Our First Building in America', in *Art and Architecture: A Symposium Hosted by The Chinati Foundation, Marfa, Texas on April 25 and 26, 1998*, Marfa, Texas 2000, p.36.

3 *Tate Gallery of Modern Art, Questionnaire*, 5 January 1994; Tate Archive, Map TG 12/4/1/15 [Architectural Competition Tate Modern Project].

4 Gerhard Richter, *Questionnaire Response [letter]*, March 8, 1994; Tate Archive, Map TG 12/4/1/16 [Architectural Competition Tate Modern Project].

5 Hal Foster, *The Art-Architecture Complex*, London 2011, p.vii.

6 Geert Bekaert, 'Art Gallery Architecture / Museum – Architectuur', in Blotkamp 1979, p.174 (author's translation).

7 Donald Judd, *Nie wieder Krieg* (1991), reproduced in Peter Noever (ed.), *Donald Judd: Architecture*, Ostfildern 2003, p.17.

8 Rachel Whiteread, *Questionnaire Response [fax]*, March 9, 1994; Tate Archive, Map TG 12/4/1/16 [Architectural Competition Tate Modern Project].

9 John Baldessari, quoted in Christina Bechtler and Dora Imhof (eds.), *Museum of the Future*, Zurich 2014, p.24.

10 Herzog & de Meuron, in *Architectures of Herzog & de Meuron; Portraits by Thomas Ruff*, New York 1994, p.47.

11 Herzog & de Meuron, 'Collaborations with Artists' 2000, p.31. The complete list is obviously much longer. Artists with whom Herzog & de Meuron have collaborated are: Helmut Federle, Rémy Zaugg, Thomas Ruff, Pipilotti Rist, Hannah Villiger, Adrian Schiess, Rosemarie Trockel, Ai Weiwei, Erik Steinbrecher, Gerda Steiner & Jörg Lenzlinger and Olafur Eliasson. Artists who have been commissioned to produce a work for one or more projects by Herzog & de Meuron are: Rémy Zaugg, Thomas Ruff, Adrian Schiess, Rosemarie Trockel, Dan Graham, Gerhard Richter, Monika Sosnowska, Erik Steinbrecher, Gerda Steiner & Jörg Lenzlinger, Olafur Eliasson, Anish Kapoor, Doug Aitken, Peter Fischli & David Weiss and Katharina Fritsch. Artists whose work and practice have served as a historical reference for the architects are Joseph Beuys and Karl Blossfeldt. Herzog & de Meuron have built artist studios for Rémy Zaugg, Thomas Ruff and Andreas Gursky. The following artists have been commissioned to depict buildings by Herzog & de Meuron: Hannah Villiger, Balthasar Burkhard, Margherita Spiluttini (Margherita Krischanitz), Thomas Ruff, Ai Weiwei, Andreas Gursky and Hiroshi Sugimoto.

12 Theodora Vischer and Jacques Herzog, 'Interview by Theodora Vischer with Jacques Herzog', in *Architectures of Herzog & de Meuron; Portraits by Thomas Ruff*, New York 1994, p.28.

13 Jorge Luis Borges, *A Compass* (translated from the Spanish by Robert Mezey), *Poetry Magazine*, June 1993, p.158.

14 Chris Dercon, in Bechtler and Imhof 2014, p.78.

15 Nicholas Serota, quoted in Cynthia C. Davidson, 'An Interview with Nicholas Serota and Richard Burdett', *Any*, no.13, 1996, p.46. For an in-depth analysis of the institutional motivations of the reconversion of Bankside Power Station, see Wouter Davidts, 'Art Factories: Museums of Contemporary Art and the Promise of Artistic Production, from Centre Pompidou to Tate Modern', *Fabrications, The Journal of the Society of Architectural Historians, Australia and New Zealand*, vol.16, no.1, 2006, pp.23–42.

16 Donald Judd, 'Marfa, Texas', in *Complete Writings 1975–1986*, Eindhoven 1986, p.102.

17 Philip Ursprung (ed.), *Herzog and de Meuron: Natural History*, Baden 2002, p.149.

18 'Herzog & de Meuron Architects, Tate Gallery of Modern Art. Competition to Select an Architect. Stage 1. Competition Entry Herzog & de Meuron Architects', Tate Archive [Architectural Competition; Stage 1], 1994.

19 Jacques Herzog in telephone conversation with the author, 19 November 2015.

20 For an overview of the designs in the different stages of the first competition, see, amongst others, Rowan Moore and Sharon Gethings, *Tate Gallery of Modern Art: Selecting an Architect*, exhibition catalogue, Tate Gallery, London 1995; Rowan Moore and Raymund Ryan, (eds.), *Building Tate Modern: Herzog & de Meuron Transforming Giles Gilbert Scott*, London 2000.

21 Herzog & de Meuron Architects, *Tate Gallery of Modern Art. Competition to Select an Architect. Stage 1. Competition Entry Herzog & de Meuron Architects*, November 7, 1994; Tate Archive, Map TG 12/4/6/13 [Architectural Competition; Stage 1].

22 Davidson 1996, p.49.

23 For an in-depth analysis of the role of the Turbine Hall within the first stage of Tate Modern, and the importance of The Unilever Series, I wish to refer to Wouter Davidts, 'A Grey Universe: Tate Modern's Turbine Hall and The Unilever Series', in Christopher Marschall (ed.), *Sculpture and the Museum*, London 2011, pp.197–216.

24 For a description of the audience behaviour, see Adrian Hardwicke, 'Secret diary of an art gallery attendant', *Guardian*, 18 March 2004.

25 *Transforming Tate Modern: A New Museum for 21st Century Britain*, press release, Tate Press Office, London, 25 July 2006.

26 'Introduction and Vision', in *Transforming Tate Modern. Coordinate Architectural and Engineering Brief*, Tate, London, October 2007, unpag.

27 Morris Hargreaves McIntire, 'Tate through Visitor's Eyes. An Anatomy of a Visit, London, January 2004', Appendix 5.0 to *Transforming Tate Modern. Coordinate Architectural and Engineering Brief*, Tate, London, 2007, unpag.

28 Chris Dercon, 'What is the Museum of the Future?', *Tate Etc.*, no.35, September 2015, p.85.

29 For this argument I am indebted to a conversation on the future role and fate of museums with Andrea Phillips, 15 September 2015.

30 Chris Dercon, in Bechtler and Imhof, *Museum of the Future*, 2014, p.71.

31 Ibid., p.72.

32 Herzog & de Meuron, TTM TTM 2, 19 January 2009; internal project report.

33 For a critical assessment of the culture of museum extension wings, I wish to refer to 'Wings That Don't Fly (And Some That Do)', in Victoria Newhouse, *Towards a New Museum*, New York 1998, pp.138–89.

34 Herzog & de Meuron, TTM TM2, 7 January 2010, internal project report.

35 During the design process, architect Yoshio Taniguchi alledgedly said to the Trustees of the New York

Museum of Modern Art: 'Raise a lot of money for me, I'll give you good architecture. Raise even more money, I'll make the architecture disappear.' Yoshio Taniguchi, quoted in John Updike, 'Invisible Cathedral: A walk through the New Modern', *The New Yorker*, 15 November 2004.
36 Jacques Herzog in telephone conversation with the author, 19 November 2015.
37 Model no.263_495-MO, viewed at the Jacques Herzog and Pierre de Meuron Kabinett (Foundation), Basel, on 9 November 2015.
38 Nikolaus Pevsner, Hugh Honour and John Fleming, *The Dictionary of Architecture and Landscape Architecture*, Munich, 1987 (London, 1966), p.701; Henri Frankfort, *The Art and Architecture of the Ancient Orient*, London 1969, pp.5–9; Th. A. Busink, 'L´origine et évolution de la ziggurat babylonienne', in *Jaarbericht van het Vooraziatisch-Egyptisch Genootschap Ex Oriente Lux* 21, 1970, pp.91–141. The building that is believed to lie at the basis of the story of the Tower of Babel is the Ziggurat of the Moon God Nanna at the city of Ur in Mesopotamia, built by King Ur-Nammu c.2100 B.C.
39 Herodotus, *The Histories, Book I*, trans. A. D. Godley, Cambridge, MA 1920, pp.178–82, http://www.perseus.tufts.edu, accessed 30 November 2015.
40 *Tate Learning Brief*, in *Transforming Tate Modern. Coordinate Architectural and Engineering Brief*, Tate, London, 2007, 4.1., n.p.
41 Ibid.
42 Edward P. Alexander, *Museums in Motion*, Nashville, Tennessee 1979, pp.6–7.
43 Jorge Luis Borges, 'The Library of Babel', in *Collected Fictions*, trans. by Andrew Hurley, New York 1998, p.118.
44 Robert Smithson, *Entropy and the New Monuments* (1966), in Jack D. Flam (ed.), *Robert Smithson: The Collected Writings*, Berkeley 1996, pp.10–23, p.11.
45 *Jacques Herzog / Pierre de Meuron / Rémy Zaugg zum Projekt 'Berlin Zentrum' 1990*, quoted in Jacques Herzog and Pierre de Meuron, *Architektur von Herzog & de Meuron fotografiert von Margherita Krischanitz, Balthasar Burkhard, Hannah Villiger und Thomas Ruff, mit einem Text von Theodora Vischer*, exh. cat., Schweizer Pavillon anlässlich der 5. internationalen Architekturausstellung der Biennale von Venedig 1991, Baden 1991, p.42: 'Die Gestalt des Hauses ist nicht die architektonische Gestaltung, die der Architekt oder der Künstler dem Haus verleiht. Es ist auch nicht die Gestaltung, die der Ökonom oder der Techniker oder der Statiker dem Haus verleiht. Es ist die Gestalt, die der Wahrnehmende dem Haus verleiht.'

Beatriz Colomina
The Museum after Art
1 Le Corbusier, *L'Esprit nouveau*, n.19, 1923.
2 Quoted in Julius Posener, 'Los primeros años: de Schinkel a De Stijl', *A&V: Monografías de Arquitectura y Vivienda*, vol.6, no.33, 1986, author's translation.
3 Colin Rowe, *As I Was Saying: Recollections and Miscellaneous Essays*, vol.I, Cambridge, MA 1996.
4 Local journalist from Barcelona reviewing the pavilion, quoted in José Quetglas, 'Fear of Glass: The Barcelona Pavilion', in Beatriz Colomina (ed.), *Revisions* 2, New York 1988, p.130.
5 Today Maison La Roche-Jeanneret is the headquarters of the Fondation Le Corbusier, a foundation and museum displaying Le Corbusier's paintings, furniture, drawings, photographs and all the documentation of his projects, as well as his correspondence, telephone bills, electricity bills, laundry bills, bank statements, postcards, suitcases and trunks, travel snapshots, family pictures, court proceedings (he was often involved in lawsuits), pottery, rugs, sea shells, pipes, books, magazines, newspaper clippings, mail order catalogues, drafts for lectures, doodles, scribbles, notebooks, sketchbooks, diaries; in short, a museum of everything.
6 Le Corbusier and Ozenfant acted as La Roche's bidders when the confiscated paintings by Picasso, Braque, Léger, and Gris from the Kahnweiler Collection at four art auctions held in June and November 1921, July 1922 and May 1923. See Russell Walden, 'New Light on Le Corbusier's Early Years in Paris: The La Roche-Jeanneret Houses', in Russell Walden (ed.), *The Open Hand: Essays on Le Corbusier*, Cambridge, MA 1977, p.135.
7 La Roche to Le Corbusier, 24 May 1926, Fondation Le Corbusier.
8 Beatriz Colomina, 'Where are We?', in Eve Blau and Nancy J. Troy (eds.), *Architecture and Cubism*, Cambridge, MA 1997.
9 Le Corbusier to Ozenfant, 16 April 1925, Fondation Le Corbusier; dossier La Roche. Quoted in Tim Benton, *The Villas of Le Corbusier: 1920–1930*, New Haven 1987, p.67.
10 'Do you recall the origin of my undertaking? "La Roche, when you have a fine collection like yours, you should also have a house built worthy of it." And my response: "Fine Jeanneret, make this house for me." Now, what happened? The house, once built, was so beautiful that on seeing it I cried: "It's almost a pity to put paintings into it!" Nevertheless I did so. How could I have done otherwise? Do I not have certain obligations with regard to my painters, of whom you yourself are one? I commissioned from you a "frame for my collection". You provided me with a "poem of walls". Which of us two is most two blame?' La Roche to Le Corbusier, 24 May 1926, Fondation Le Corbusier. Quoted in ibid., p.70.
11 'L'architecture arabe nous donne un enseignement précieux. Elle s'apprécie *à la marche*, avec le pied; c'est en marchant, en se déplaçant que l'on voit se développer les ordonnances de l'architecture. C'est un principe contraire à l'architecture baroque qui est conçue sur le papier, autour d'un point fixe théorique. Je préfère l'enseignement de l'architecture arabe. Dans cette maison-ci, il s'agit d'une véritable promenade architecturale, offrant des aspects constamment variés, inattendus, parfois étonnants.' Le Corbusier and Jeanneret, *Œuvre Complète*, vol.2, 1929–34, Zurich 1964, p.24.
12 Le Corbusier, *Precisions*, Paris 1930, p.136.
13 Mies van der Rohe's houses likewise act as the basis of a radical proposal for a new kind of museum, as with the Museum for a Small City in 1942, a project that stands with Le Corbusier's Museum of Unlimited Growth as the two most significant proposals for museums of the modern movement. See Beatriz Colomina, 'The Endless Museum: Le Corbusier and Mies van der Rohe', in *When Things Cast No Shadow*, exh. cat., 5th Berlin Biennial for Contemporary Art, Berlin 2008.
14 Paul Otlet, UAI (Union of International Associations) 1925, p.4. Promotional booklet, quoted in Michael Raeburn and Victoria Wilson (eds.), *Le Corbusier: Architect of the Century*, exh. cat., Hayward Gallery, London 1987, p.165.
15 'Le musée n'a pas de façade; le visiteur ne verra jamais de façade; il ne verra que l'intérieur du musée. Car il entra au cœur du musée par un souterrain dont la porte d'entrée est ouvert dans un mur qui, si le musée arrivait a une étape de croissance magnifique, offrirait à ce moment le neuf millième mètre de cimaise.'
16 Le Corbusier to M. Zervos, 8 December 1930, in *Cahiers d'art*, reprinted in Le Corbusier and Pierre Jeanneret, *Œuvre Complète*, vol.2, 1929–34, Zurich 1964, p.73. English translation in W. Boesiger and H. Girsberger (eds.), *Le Corbusier 1910–65*, Zurich 1967, p.236.
16 Le Corbusier, *My Work*, trans. by James Palmes, London 1960, p.101.
17 See note 1.
18 Prithwish Neogy, Director, *Brochure for the Cultural Centre*, Ahmedabad. Quoted in Raeburn and Wilson 1987, p.301.
19 Ibid.
20 Le Corbusier and Jeanneret, *Œuvre Complète*, vol.7, 1957–65, Zurich, p.163. Le Corbusier presents the project in a book entitled *Le Musée du XXe siècle*, showing how this project is to be positioned on a key node in a transnational network. Ibid., pp.164–77.
21 'Wright Versus Painting: The Guggenheim Museum', *The New York Times*, 21 October 1959.
22 Frank Lloyd Wright, 'The Solomon R. Guggenheim Museum', text dated June 1958, in Bruce Brooks Pfeiffer (ed.), *Frank Lloyd Wright Collected Writings*, New York 1995, vol.5, p.248.
23 Walter Benjamin, *The Arcades Project*, Harvard, 2002, p.3.

Select Bibliography

2000

Hubertus Adam, 'Südlich der Themse. Umbau der Bankside Power Station zur neuen Tate Gallery', *Bauwelt*, no.23, 16 June 2000, pp.26–33

Wolfgang Bachmann, 'Tate', *Baumeister*, no.6, 2000, pp.20–35

Dominique Boudet, 'Herzog & de Meuron Tate Modern Londres', in *AMC Le Moniteur Architecture*, vol.108, June 2000. pp.53–69

Tony Fretton, 'Into the Void: Herzog & de Meuron's Tate Modern', *Architecture Today*, no.109, June 2000, pp.34–42

Brian Hatton, 'Fatto alla grande. The biggest way to do art', *Lotus*, no.106, 2000, pp.6–34

Jacques Herzog, Nicholas Serota, Rowan Moore, 'Conversation. Jacques Herzog, Nicholas Serota, Rowan Moore, August 1999', in Rowan Moore & Raymud Ryan, *Building Tate Modern. Herzog & de Meuron transforming Giles Gilbert Scott*, London: Tate Gallery Publishing Ltd., 2000, pp.37–57

Herzog & de Meuron, *Herzog & de Meuron: 11 Stations. An Architectural Narrative*, exh. cat., London: Tate, 2000

Herzog & de Meuron, 'Herzog & de Meuron: Tate Modern, Bankside Power Station', in Yoshio Futagawa (ed.), *GA Document*, vol.62, July 2000, pp.10–33

'Herzog & de Meuron. Bauen für die Welt', *Du. Die Zeitschrift der Kultur*, no.706, May 2000, pp.6–61

Jeffrey Kipnis, 'Die List der Kosmetik', in *Du. Die Zeitschrift der Kultur*, no.706, May 2000, pp.6–44

Alice Rawsthorn, 'Shining examples of the architect's art', *Financial Times*, London, 17 May 2000, p.iv

Alice Rawsthorn, 'The Tate's own masterpiece', *Financial Times*, 13 May 2000, p.7

Peter Schjeldahl, 'The Tate Trip: Modernism revised on the Thames', *The New Yorker*, 29 May 2000

'Tate Modern: The conversion of the industrial scale', *Space Design*, no.433, October 2000, pp.52–3

'Tate Modern in London', *Detail. Zeitschrift für Architektur und Baudetail. Review of Architecture. Umnutzung, Ergänzung, Sanierung*, no.7, Oct. 2000, pp.1251–61

'Tate Modern, London. Ein Kraftwerk für die Kunst – gekonnt in Szene gesetzt', *Werk, Bauen + Wohnen*, no.10, 2000

2001

Mignon Nixon et al., 'Round Table: Tate Modern (7 May 2001)', *October 98*, Fall 2001, pp.3–25

2002

Richard Burdett, 'Stadt am Fluss. Stadterneuerung in London', *Deutsche Bauzeitung*, no.2, 2002, pp.42–51

2003

Hugh Muir, 'Tate leads Fight to halt Tower. Serota heads Bankside Protesters attempting to stop Building of 20-Storey Apartment Block but Livingstone backs Developer', *Guardian*, 9 July 2003, p.9

Christian Schittich, 'Tate Modern in London: Architekten Herzog & de Meuron, Basel', *Bauen im Bestand. Umnutzung, Ergänzung, Neuschöpfung*, Munich: Ed. Detail, 2003, pp.136–43

2004

Carla Bertolucci & Rob Gregory, 'Bankside Revisited', *The Architectural Review*, no.1288, June 2004, pp.80–1

2005

Rowan Moore, 'Architecture in Motion', in Tate Trustees 2005 (eds.), *Tate Modern: The First Five Years*, London, Tate, 2005, pp.29–32

Tate Trustees (eds.), *Tate Modern: The First Five Years*, London, Tate, 2005

2006

Peter Aspden, 'How a Talent for Spectacle gives Tate Modern its Edge', *Financial Times*, 29 July 2006, p.7

Edwin Heathcote, 'Tate Masterplan for a glittering Future', *Financial Times*, 26 July 2006, p.9

Jacques Herzog & Ulrike Zophoniasson-Baierl, 'Die Stadt ist eine ewige Baustelle. Jacques Herzog will die Idee der Tate Modern zu Ende denken, aber keinesfalls für alle Zeiten', *Basler Zeitung*, 8 Aug. 2006, *Kulturmagazin* supplement, pp.4–5

Emily King & Angus Hyland, *C/id: Visual Identity and Branding for the Arts*, London, Laurence King, 2006

Alexander Menden, 'Ich möchte zu Fuss nach Southwark gehen. Agenda 2012: Die Architekten Herzog & de Meuron erweitern die Londoner Tate Modern', in *Süddeutsche Zeitung*, 27 July 2006, p.13

Rowan Moore, 'A Glass Pyramid for Tate Modern', *Evening Standard*, 25 July 2006, p.39

Rowan Moore, 'The Proposed Film', *Evening Standard*, 25 July 2006

Deyan Sudjic, 'Extension for the House that Jacques and Pierre built', *Observer*, 30 July 2006, p.10

2007

Wouter Davidts, 'The Vast and the Void: On Tate Modern's Turbine Hall and "The Unilever Series"', *Footprint: Delft School of Design Journal*, Autumn 2007, pp.77–92

Gunther Vögt, *Miniature and Panorama: Vogt landscape architects*, Zürich: Lars Müller Publishers, 2007 (new edition 2012)

2008

Olafur Eliasson, 2003, Turbine Hall, Tate Modern, London (The Unilever Series), 2003, *Lotus*, no.135, 2008, p.123.

2009

T.J. Demos, 'The Tate Effect', in Hans Belting, Andrea Buddensieg & Peter Weibel (eds.), *Where is Art Contemporary? The Global Art World*, no.2, Karlsruhe: ZKM | Center for Art and Media, 2009, pp.78–87

2010

'The ever-expanding Tate', *The Burlington Magazine*, 1 Oct. 2010

Philip Ursprung, 'Container: Rückgrat der Globalisierung', in *Global Design: Internationale Perspektiven und individuelle Konzepte*, exh. cat., Museum für Gestaltung Zürich, Baden: Lars Müller Publishers, 2010, pp.122–33

2012

Claire Bishop, *Artificial Hells: Participatory Art and the Politics of Spectatorship*, London: Verso, 2012

Angelus Eichinger, Jörg Seifert & Harry Gugger, 'Von Rollenspielen, verschleierter Monumentalität und Arm's-Length Bodies. Tate Modern im Bankside-Kraftwerk, London' ['On Role Play, hidden Monumentality, and Arm's-Length Bodies. Tate Modern in Bankside Power Station, London'], in A. Eichinger & J. Seifert (eds.), *UrbanRESET. Freilegen immanenter Potenziale städtischer Räume/How to Activate Immanent Potentials of Urban Spaces*, Basel: Birkhäuser GmbH, 2012, pp.112–27

Jacques Herzog, 'From an Industrial Underground. Architect Jacques Herzog recalls his first Visit to the Tanks and explains how their sinister, dark rawness continues to shape and inspire Tate Modern', in *The Tanks at Tate Modern. Fifteen Weeks of Art in Action. 18 July – 28 October 2012. The Tanks Programme Notes*, exh. cat., London: Tate, 2012, pp.34–5

Rowan Moore, 'Two Decades of Herzog & de Meuron', *The Architectural Review*, March 2015, pp.79–89

Rowan Moore, 'It may just look like a lot of old concrete, but the conversion of the oil tanks beneath Tate Modern is a work of art in its own right', *Observer*, 1 July 2012, p.30

Nicholas Serota, 'The Tanks I', *Tate Etc*, no.25, 2012, pp.58–9.

Calvin Tomkins, 'The Modern Man: How the Tate Gallery's Nicholas Serota is Reinventing the Museum', *The New Yorker*, 2 July 2012

2013

Miguel Amado, 'Tate Modern and *Century City*: Two Sides of the Same Coin', *The Exhibitionist*, no.7, 2013, pp.12–15

Hal Foster, *The Art-Architecture Complex*, London / New York, Verso, 2013, pp.123–9

Jessica Morgan & Ann Temkin, 'The Museum as Spectacle', *Mousse* no.38, April 2013, pp.188–93

2014

Cristina Bechtler (ed.), *Museum of the Future*, Zurich, Dijon, 2014

Beatriz Colomina, 'Collaboration in Modern Architecture', *The Berlin Journal*, no.27, Fall 2014, pp.26–9

Guido Guerzoni (ed.), *Museums on the Map 1995–2012*, Turin: Umberto Allemandi & Co., 2014, pp.45–72. (pp.45–9 ['Size Analysis', 'Design and Construction Time'], 52–3 ['Cost Analysis', 'Cost Analysis per Square Metre'], 58–9 ['Average Cost per Square Meter Divided by Year'], 64–5 ['Architects'], 71 ['Top 23 Most Active architects'], 72 ['Average Cost per Square Metre of Museums by the Top 17 Architects'])

2015

Rebecca Bornhauser & Thomas Kissling, '"Open space is the city's most important resource": On the difficult relationship between the city and landscape', in G. Vogt, R. Bornhauser & T. Kissling (eds.), *Landschaft als Wunderkammer: fragen nacht einer Haltung* [*Landscape as a Cabinet of Curiosities: In search of a position*], Zürich: Lars Müller Publishers, 2015, pp.45–90

Chris Dercon et al., 'What is the Museum of the Future?', *Tate Etc*, no.35, Autumn 2015, pp.82–92

Hal Foster, 'After the White Cube', *London Review of Books*, vol.37, no.6, 19 March 2015, pp.25–6

Hal Foster, *Bad New Days: Art, Criticism, Emergency*, London: Verso, 2015

Jasper Morrison, *A Book of Things*, Zürich: Lars Müller Publishers, 2015

'Tate Modern. Herzog & de Meuron. Bankside, Southwark 2000', *Architecture and Urbanism*, vol.536, May 2015, pp.108–9

Kali Tzortzi, 'Building meaning: How architecture affects our experience of museums', *ICOM News: The International Council of Museums Magazine*, vol.68, no.2, Sept. 2015, pp.8–9

Günther Vogt, Rebecca Bornhauser, Thomas Kissling, *Landscape as a Cabinet of Curiosities*, Zürich: Lars Müller Publishers, 2015

2016

Vladimir Gintoff, 'What Tate Modern Means in a Post-Brexit World', *Metropolis*, New York, 7 July 2016

Marion Löhndorf, 'Der neu eröffnete Erweitrungsbau der Tate Modern. In der welt verankert', *Neue Zuercher Zeitung*, 17 June 2016

Rowan Moore, 'Herzog and De Meuron: Tate Modern's architects on their radical new extension', *Guardian*, 15 May 2016

Rowan Moore, *Slow Burn City: London in the twenty-first century*, London: Picador, 2016

Hanno Rauterberg, 'Da drecht sich was', *Die Zeit*, 30 June 2016

Eva Steidl, 'Die Neue Moderne', *Domus*, 20 July / August 2016

Günther Vogt (ed.), *Wunderlust/Wanderkammer*, Zürich: Lars Müller Publishers, 2016

Oliver Wainwright, 'First look inside the Switch House – Tate Modern's power pyramid', *Guardian*, 23 May 2016

Oliver Wainwright, 'How we made Tate Modern', interviews with Jacques Herzog and Pierre de Meuron, and with Nicholas Serota, *Guardian*, 21 June 2016

Jackie Wullschlager, 'How Tate Modern transformed the way we see art', *Financial Times*, 27 May 2016

Acknowledgements

This book records the achievements of hundreds of individuals in creating a museum of modern and contemporary art for London over a period of nearly twenty-five years. It has been a collective effort by successive Boards of Trustees, their Chairmen, the directors and staff of Tate Modern, the staff of Tate as a whole, advisers on fundraising, building and communication, friends in the political world of London and the nation and members of the public whose regular comments on Tate keep informed about their needs.

Amongst all these people, a small group has guided the creation of the second phase of the building. The Tate Modern Project Board has been chaired by Christopher Jonas, who served in a similar capacity on the original building. We, and all visitors in the future, owe him an enormous debt of gratitude for his work over a period of twenty years. In this phase, he has been assisted at every turn by a small committee comprising Roger Madelin, Paul Morrell and Keith Salway, who have brought to our project their great experience of commissioning and accounting for cost on large buildings. Throughout the creation of Tate Modern the residents of Bankside and the communities of Southwark have given immense support to the project. In this phase the Leader of Southwark Council, Peter John, has been closely involved, while Adele Morris has kindly chaired the Tate Modern Community Liaison Group and Peter Williams, Chief Executive of Better Bankside, has given invaluable counsel to Tate.

The consultants and contractors who have worked to design and realise Tate Modern are listed in the Facts and Figures section, but the Trustees would like to express special thanks to the senior teams at Herzog & de Meuron (Jacques Herzog, Pierre de Meuron, Ascan Mergenthaler, John O'Mara, and at the outset Michael Casey, former associate, and Harry Gugger, former partner at Herzog & de Meuron); Vogt (Günther Vogt); Ramboll UK, AECOM (Peter Flint); Max Fordham & Partners; GTMS; Stanhope; Cartlidge Levene (Ian Cartlidge); Jasper Morrison Studio (Jasper Morrison and John Tree); Bolton & Quinn (Erica Bolton) and their supporting consultant teams. The principal contractor, Mace, has faced the challenge of realising a complex building and our thanks are due in particular to Mark Reynolds and Mark Castle.

The team at Tate has been led successively by Alex Beard as Deputy Director until 2013 and since then by Kerstin Mogull, Managing Director, supported by Stephen Wingfield. Jo Dunnett was the project director almost from start to finish, managing not just the building but valiantly addressing all the issues associated with creating a new museum. Donald Hyslop, as Head of Regeneration and Community Partnerships since 2001, has worked closely with local residents and the community. Very sadly, Rebecca Williams, Director of Audiences & Development, did not have the opportunity to see the completion of the edifice for which she had done so much to raise funds, but her achievements will be remembered in perpetuity.

The book would not have been possible without the help of many people who worked behind the scenes and often beyond the call of duty. They are too numerous to acknowledge individually, but we would like to thank in particular, in addition to those mentioned above: the teams at Herzog & de Meuron – the active Tate Project team in London as well as the Archives team in Basel; Andrew Dunkley and Marcus Leith in the Tate Photography department; Jo Dunnett, Rebecca Evans and Magdalena Maculewicz in the Tate Project team; Roanne Marner and Emma O'Neill at Tate Publishing; Laure Baretaud at Vogt; and James Sutton at Peter Willberg's studio.

For James Morris's photographic shoot we are very grateful to Alex Crabtree, Brian Ewin, Stuart Gumbrell, Stefania Mosca, Robyn Ranu and Fabio Valencia for facilitating access to neighbouring buildings; and to Gafar Bello and Steve Rozee for helping with logistics at Tate Modern.

We would like to acknowledge and thank the following benefactors who have supported Tate Modern Capital campaigns.

Tate Modern Donors to the Founding Capital Campaign
29th May 1961 Charitable Trust
AMP
The Annenberg Foundation
Arts Council England
The Asprey Family
    Charitable Foundation
Lord and Lady Attenborough
The Baring Foundation
Ron Beller and Jennifer Moses
Alex and Angela Bernstein
David and Janice Blackburn
Mr and Mrs Anthony Bloom
BNP Paribas
Mr and Mrs Pontus Bonnier
Lauren and Mark Booth
Mr and Mrs John Botts
Frances and John Bowes
Ivor Braka
Mr and Mrs James Brice
The British Land Company plc
Donald L Bryant Jr Family
Melva Bucksbaum
Cazenove & Co
The Clore Duffield Foundation
CGU plc
Clifford Chance
Edwin C Cohen
The John S Cohen Foundation
Ronald and Sharon Cohen
Sadie Coles
Carole and Neville Conrad
Giles and Sonia Coode-Adams
Douglas Cramer
Alan Cristea Gallery
Thomas Dane
Michel and Hélène David-Weill
Julia W Dayton
Gilbert de Botton
Pauline Denyer-Smith and Paul Smith
Sir Harry and Lady Djanogly
The Drapers' Company
Energis Communications
English Heritage
English Partnerships
The Eranda Foundation
Esmée Fairbairn Charitable Trust
Donald and Doris Fisher
Richard B and Jeanne Donovan Fisher
The Fishmongers' Company
Freshfields Bruckhaus Deringer
Friends of the Tate Gallery
Bob and Kate Gavron
Giancarlo Giammetti
Alan Gibbs
Mr and Mrs Edward Gilhuly
GKR
GLG Partners
Helyn and Ralph Goldenberg
Goldman Sachs
The Horace W Goldsmith Foundation

The Worshipful Company
    of Goldsmiths
Lydia and Manfred Gorvy
Noam and Geraldine Gottesman
Pehr and Christina Gyllenhammar
Mimi and Peter Haas
The Worshipful Company
    of Haberdashers
Hanover Acceptances Limited
The Headley Trust
Mr and Mrs André Hoffmann
Anthony and Evelyn Jacobs
Jay Jopling
Mr and Mrs Karpidas
Howard and Lynda Karshan
Peter and Maria Kellner
Madeleine Kleinwort
Brian and Lesley Knox
Pamela and C Richard Kramlich
Mr and Mrs Henry R Kravis
Irene and Hyman Kreitman
The Kresge Foundation
Catherine and Pierre Lagrange
The Lauder Foundation – Leonard and
    Evelyn Lauder Fund
Lazard Brothers & Co., Limited
Leathersellers' Company
    Charitable Fund
Edward and Agnès Lee
Lex Service Plc
Lehman Brothers
Ruth and Stuart Lipton
Anders and Ulla Ljungh
The Frank Lloyd Family Trusts
London & Cambridge
    Properties Limited
London Electricity plc, EDF Group
Mr and Mrs George Loudon
Mayer, Brown, Rowe & Maw
Viviane and James Mayor
Ronald and Rita McAulay
The Mercers' Company
The Meyer Foundation
The Millennium Commission
Anthony and Deirdre Montagu
The Monument Trust
Mori Building, Ltd
Mr and Mrs M D Moross
Guy and Marion Naggar
Peter and Eileen Norton,
    The Peter Norton
    Family Foundation
Maja Oeri and Hans Bodenmann
Sir Peter and Lady Osborne
William A Palmer
Mr Frederik Paulsen
Pearson plc
The Pet Shop Boys
The Nyda and
    Oliver Prenn Foundation
Prudential plc
Railtrack plc
The Rayne Foundation
Reuters
Sir John and Lady Ritblat
Rolls-Royce plc
Barrie and Emmanuel Roman
Lord and Lady Rothschild

The Dr Mortimer and Theresa Sackler
    Foundation
J. Sainsbury plc
Ruth and Stephan Schmidheiny
Schroders
Mr and Mrs Charles Schwab
David and Sophie Shalit
Belle Shenkman Estate
William Sieghart
Peter Simon
Mr and Mrs Sven Skarendahl
London Borough of Southwark
The Foundation for Sports
    and the Arts
Mr and Mrs Nicholas Stanley
The Starr Foundation
The Jack Steinberg Charitable Trust
Charlotte Stevenson
Hugh and Catherine Stevenson
John Studzinski
David and Linda Supino
The Government of Switzerland
Carter and Mary Thacher
Insinger Townsley
UBS
UBS Warburg
David and Emma Verey
Dinah Verey
The Vintners' Company
Clodagh and Leslie Waddington
Robert and Felicity Waley-Cohen
Wasserstein, Perella & Co., Inc.
Gordon D Watson
The Weston Family
Mr and Mrs Stephen Wilberding
Michael S Wilson
Poju and Anita Zabludowicz

and those donors who wish
to remain anonymous

Donors to The Tate Modern Project
Artist Rooms Foundation
Abigail and Joseph Baratta
Blavatnik Family Foundation
Lauren and Mark Booth
The Deborah Loeb Brice Foundation
The Lord Browne of Madingley,
    FRS, FREng
John and Michael Chandris,
    and Christina Chandris
James Chanos
Paul Cooke
The Roger De Haan Charitable Trust
Ago Demirdjian and Tiqui Atencio
    Demirdjian
Department for Culture,
    Media and Sport
George Economou
Stefan Edlis and Gael Neeson
English Partnerships
Mrs Donald B Fisher
Jeanne Donovan Fisher
Mala Gaonkar
The Ghandehari Foundation
Thomas Gibson in memory
    of Anthea Gibson
Lydia and Manfred Gorvy

Noam Gottesman
The Hayden Family Foundation
Peter and Maria Kellner
Madeleine Kleinwort
Catherine Lagrange
Pierre Lagrange
London Development Agency
LUMA Foundation
Allison and Howard W Lutnick
Donald B Marron
Scott and Suling Mead
Anthony and Deirdre Montagu
Mrs Yoshiko Mori
Elisabeth Murdoch
The Eyal Ofer Family Foundation
Maureen Paley
Simon and Midge Palley
Stephen and Yana Peel
Daniel and Elizabeth Peltz
Catherine Petitgas
Franck Petitgas
Barrie and Emmanuel Roman
The Dr Mortimer and
    Theresa Sackler Foundation
The Sackler Trust
Stephan Schmidheiny Family/
    Daros Collection
London Borough of Southwark
John J Studzinski, CBE
Tate Americas Foundation
Tate Members
Julie-Anne Uggla
Lance Uggla
Viktor Vekselberg
Nina and Graham Williams
Manuela and Iwan Wirth
The Wolfson Foundation

and those who wish to remain
anonymous

Biographical Notes

Ian Cartlidge founded London-based design studio Cartlidge Levene in 1987, specialising in the creation of identity and visual language. The studio has developed wayfinding schemes for Tate Modern as well as many major museums, galleries, schools and sporting arenas, and has worked with some of the world's leading architects. Its most significant projects include the Barbican Centre, Guardian News and Media, Royal College of Art, Selfridges & Co and the Victoria & Albert Museum. Ian was awarded the distinction of Royal Designer for Industry (RDI) in 2013 by the RSA.

Beatriz Colomina is founding director of the Program in Media and Modernity at Princeton University and Professor in the School of Architecture. She has written extensively on questions of architecture, art, sexuality and media. Her books include *Manifesto Architecture: The Ghost of Mies* (2014), *Clip/Stamp/Fold: The Radical Architecture of Little Magazines 196X–197X* (2010), *Domesticity at War* (2007), *Privacy and Publicity: Modern Architecture as Mass Media* (1994), and *Sexuality and Space* (1992). She has curated a number of exhibitions including *Clip/Stamp/Fold* (2006), *Playboy Architecture* (2012) and *Radical Pedagogies* (2014). She is curator (with Mark Wigley) of the third Istanbul Design Biennial (2016).

Wouter Davidts is Adjunct-Professor at the Department of Architecture and Urban Planning at Ghent University and teaches at Sint Lucas School of Arts, Antwerp and the Drama Department of the Royal Conservatory, Antwerp. He has held research fellowships at Goldsmiths, London, Avans University in the Netherlands, and the Henry Moore Institute, Leeds. He has written widely on the museum, contemporary art and architecture. His books include *Bouwen voor de kunst? Museumarchitectuur van Centre Pompidou tot Tate Modern* (2006) and *Triple Bound. Art, Architecture and the Museum* (2016).

Chris Dercon was Director of Tate Modern 2010–16 and from 2017 will be at Berlin's experimental Volksbuhne Theatre. An art historian, documentary filmmaker and cultural producer, he worked on exhibitions with graphic designer Gorik Lindemans in Belgium in the 1980s, and with Walter Nikkels and others on the Witte de With *Cahiers* in Rotterdam in the 1990s. He became Director of Museum Boijmans Van Beuningen, Rotterdam in 1996, working with Robbrecht en Daem on the extension of the museum: while in Rotterdam he advised Rem Koolhaas's Office for Metropolitan Architecture on museum infrastructures. As Director of Haus Der Kunst, Munich 2003–11, Dercon developed exhibitions of Droog Design, Konstantin Grcic, Herzog & de Meuron, Rem Koolhaas and Carlo Mollino.

Herzog & de Meuron is an architectural partnership led by Jacques Herzog and Pierre de Meuron with Senior Partners Christine Binswanger, Ascan Mergenthaler and Stefan Marbach. Established in Basel in 1978, the practice has grown over the years to an international team working worldwide. The practice is renowned for cultural projects and collaborations with artists, including the Goetz Collection in Munich (1992), Schaulager Basel/Münchenstein (2003), National Stadium Beijing (2008) and Elbphilharmonie Hamburg (2017) among many others. Herzog and de Meuron have won numerous awards including The Pritzker Architecture Prize (2001), the RIBA Royal Gold Medal and the Praemium Imperiale (2007).

Jasper Morrison is founder and Director of Jasper Morrison Ltd, which is based in London and Paris. He studied at Kingston Polytechnic and the Royal College of Art in London. Since the late 1980s he has collaborated with some of the world's outstanding producers of furniture and domestic utensils, including Cappellini, Alessi, Vitra, Muji, Rosenthal, Rowenta and Flos. The two Tate Modern projects are his only commissions for public buildings in the UK.

Nicholas Serota has been Director of Tate since 1988. In this period Tate has broadened its field of interest to include twentieth-century photography, film and performance as well as collecting from Latin America, Asia, the Middle East and Africa. He recently co-curated exhibitions at Tate Modern on Cy Twombly and Gerhard Richter as well as *Henri Matisse: the Cut Outs*. He was a member of the Commission for Architecture and the Built Environment, and of the Olympic Delivery Authority, responsible for building the Olympic Park in East London for 2012.

Günther Vogt founded Vogt Landscape in 2000. Today he develops national and international projects with some forty employees in Zürich, London and Berlin, often in collaboration with high profile architectural firms. These include Herzog & de Meuron, Peter Zumthor Architects , David Chipperfield Architects, Frank Gehry Partners, Meili Peter Architects, Fletcher Priest Architects and many others. Vogt has worked with artists including Sol Lewitt, Hamish Fulton, Olafur Eliasson, Laurie Anderson, Julian Charrière and Dan Graham. Günther Vogt is also Professor for Landscape Architecture at the Swiss Federal Institute of Technology (ETH) in Zürich. In the autumn of 2012 he was visiting professor at the Harvard Graduate School of Design.

Oliver Wainwright is the architecture and design critic of the *Guardian*. After training as an architect at the University of Cambridge and the Royal College of Art, he worked in practices including OMA in Rotterdam, muf in London, and the Greater London Authority's Architecture and Urbanism Unit. He has written extensively on architecture and design for *Building Design*, the *Architects' Journal*, *Icon*, *Domus*, *Frieze* and many others. He has served as curatorial advisor to the Architecture Foundation and is a visiting critic and lecturer at architecture schools, including Harvard, Yale and the Architectural Association.